THE ART OF THE ENNEAGRAM

9 PATHS TO AWARENESS, ACCEPTANCE AND TRANSFORMATION

BY GINGER LAPID-BOGDA PHD & RUSSELL (TRES) BOGDA

ILLUSTRATIONS BY CLAIRE MCCRACKEN

The Art of the Enneagram
9 paths to awareness, acceptance and transformation

ISBN: 978-1-0879-0866-3

The Enneagram In Business Press
Albany, California
310.829.3309

www.TheEnneagramInBusiness.com

Dedicated to Eric Corso,
a beautiful spirit gone too soon

TABLE OF CONTENTS

ACKNOWLEDGEMENTS

Several people have been instrumental to this book, in particular, Anne Mureé, Enneagram teacher, colleague and dear friend. One day several months ago, Anne suggested that we write a new book on the Enneagram itself, one that would be modern in presentation and rich in insights and understanding, a great asset for anyone of any age in learning the Enneagram, from millennials and beyond. This is that book and, without Anne's gentle suggestion, this book would not have been written.

Also to be acknowledged is Chloé Keric-Eli, who enthusiastically shared her delight with the book and its contents, as well as Monirah Womack, who laughed aloud as she heard what was to be inside. No book has light shining through it without really good copyediting. Thanks to Steven Ellison and Kim Moran Davis for this. We credit Jerry Wagner for his insightful names for the 9 types used throughout the book – The Good Person (type 1), The Loving Person (type 2) and so on – and Byron Katie for the four transformative questions for type 6. In addition, and as always, credit for our foundational understanding goes to Claudio Naranjo, Don Riso, Helen Palmer and others.

Of course, our talented illustrator Claire McCracken integrated our concept into images that are simply amazing. Tres Bogda worked extensively with her to help create the book in its present form.

FROM TRES | WHY I CO-WROTE THIS BOOK

As a 29-year-old millennial and having grown up with the Enneagram since I was 5, I thought I was in a perfect place to help architect this book. My feel for the Enneagram, both inside and out, has grown and developed with time. Working with a talented team, I am beyond grateful for their dedication to this book. I am especially thankful to my friend, Claire McCracken, who took our ideas and brought them to life. She was able to artistically illuminate each type in a magnificent journey; I feel this book both describes, and artistically portrays, the beautiful paths of each type. In a time when the world greatly needs more understanding, compassion, and awareness, I hope this book opens your inner self and helps you connect to your deeper essence.

FROM GINGER | WHY I CO-WROTE THIS BOOK

How many people get the opportunity of a lifetime to create something of contribution and value with one of their children? Those of you who know me at all know how much I love and respect my son. Tres has been an ideal collaborator, with his keen mind, edgy wit, and intrinsic knowledge of the Enneagram, not to mention his age being perfect for making this book also appealing to multiple generations.

We wrote different parts of the book, always using the other as a sounding board, reviewer and editor. The more we created, the more enthused we became. Yes, a lot of hard work and dedication went into this, but fun throughout the process and deep satisfaction were the result. We hope this is a book for all ages!

INTRODUCTION

> "What you seek is seeking you." ~ Rumi

Are you curious about yourself and others? Do you wonder why some people seem so similar to one another or why some people seem so different from you, yet you somehow understand them? Do you feel drawn to certain energetic ways of being in people and not at all to others? Have you noticed that some things are really easy for you, yet hard for others and vice versa? Do some people seem to 'trigger' you in ways that other people do not?

If you answered yes to any of these questions, then you are ready to embark on an incredible path to know yourself at a deeper level and to truly understand others better and to accept them for who they are, not who you want them to be?

WHAT THE ENNEAGRAM IS AND IS NOT

The Enneagram is ancient in wisdom yet modern in usage, like an ocean alive and changing in its composition. Like the ocean, the Enneagram is dynamic, profound and powerful. It is also amazingly accurate in the way it describes the 9 different human 'characters' or human archetypes. Even more, the Enneagram dives deep into each type's thinking, feeling and behavioral patterns, as well as their motivational structure. In short, the Enneagram illuminates and is illuminating.

WHAT THE ENNEAGRAM IS	WHAT THE ENNEAGRAM IS NOT
A road to self-acceptance	A process for self-negation
A path for expansion	A method for stereotyping people
A deep inner journey	A party game
An in-depth self-study	A quick learn
A non-ending development path	A fast fix
A process for transforming self	A way to manipulate others
A deep exploration of both ego and essence	A simplistic personality system
An opportunity to develop community: the 'we'	Only about 'me'

WHERE THE ENNEAGRAM COMES FROM

No one knows the exact roots of the Enneagram. We do believe that it has been evolving over 4000 years or more, first as the circle representing the unity of all humankind; then with the triangle added; next came another element of the symbol, the hexad, that contains 6 points; and, finally, the arrow lines that connect the type numbers. Current research on the Enneagram's origins indicates it comes originally from the Middle East, most likely where the Tigris and Euphrates rivers meet.

BEFORE YOU READ THIS BOOK

You likely know just about everything necessary to read this book. And what you might not know yet is explained in the body of the book or later in the appendix. That said, there are two areas that might be useful:

YOUR ENNEAGRAM TYPE

There are 9 Enneagram types, and you have one and only one place or type number on the Enneagram. In addition, your Enneagram type remains the same throughout your lifetime. And although we don't change types – even if we desire to do so, no type is better than any other type – if we learn from self-reflection and experience, we can grow and even transform into a higher and more expanded version of our truest, deepest and best self.

CENTERS OF INTELLIGENCE

The Enneagram is based partly on the ancient wisdom that each of us has three different Centers of Intelligence – Head Center, Heart Center and Body Center – with each Center having a specific function: Head Center for rational processing; Heart Center for emotional responsiveness; and Body Center for somatic knowing. Knowing your Enneagram type illuminates how you use each Center of Intelligence, plus what you can do to increase your productive use of each Center.

Even more central to this particular book, the Centers of Intelligence inform us about something else unique to the Enneagram. Each Center of Intelligence is associated with one of the four primary human emotions: anger (for the Body Center), joy (not associated with any Center), sorrow (for the Heart Center) and fear (for the Head Center). Within the Enneagram, three of the 9 types – types 8, 9 and 1 – are formed in the Body Center of Intelligence, sharing anger as their common emotion, but with three unique ways of manifesting it. Three of the 9 types are formed in the Heart Center – types 2, 3 and 4 – and share sorrow as their common emotion, but with three distinctive ways of dealing with it. The remaining three types – types 5, 6 and 7 – are formed in the Head Center, with fear as their common emotion, but with three very different ways of responding to it. These Center-based emotional response patterns are interwoven through the sections on each type.

HOW TO READ THIS BOOK

You can read this book any way you desire. We recommend reading about the journey of each type in order – the book contains 12 pages for each type – yet it is important for you to read in your own way. We are all different, and we all learn differently.

We've written and designed this book to integrate accurate information about each Enneagram type with compelling graphics that illuminate meaning and help many people retrain what they learn. Some of us learn better visually; some from reading words, and some learn best from both.

We've used carefully chosen metaphors throughout the book, as you'll soon see: animals, exotic fruits, colors, musical references, essential oils, social media acronyms, and more. These are not meant to be taken lightly or literally; they are intended as a way to enhance understanding at a deeper and, hopefully, more memorable level. Research shows that people often remember metaphors more than words alone. You'll also find poems by Rumi – the 13th century mystic poet – throughout as well as quotes from Brené Brown and Dolly Parton. All of these are strategically placed to heighten and reinforce the concepts you're reading.

WHAT'S IN THE APPENDIX

The appendix contains four key areas: (1) three questions to ask yourself to confirm your type; (2) charts to clarify confusions between types; (3) a structural overview of the Enneagram framework; and (4) levels of self-mastery and type.

WHAT TO EXPECT NEXT

Welcome to your Enneagram journey! Here's what you can expect from working with the Enneagram: increased self-awareness; heightened self-acceptance; reduced stress; targeted self-development; strengthened psychological well-being; deeper levels of compassion; greater access to the spiritual domain; enhanced professional skills; and better relationships with other people. Think of the Enneagram as your guide.

ENNEAGRAM ONE

THE GOOD PERSON

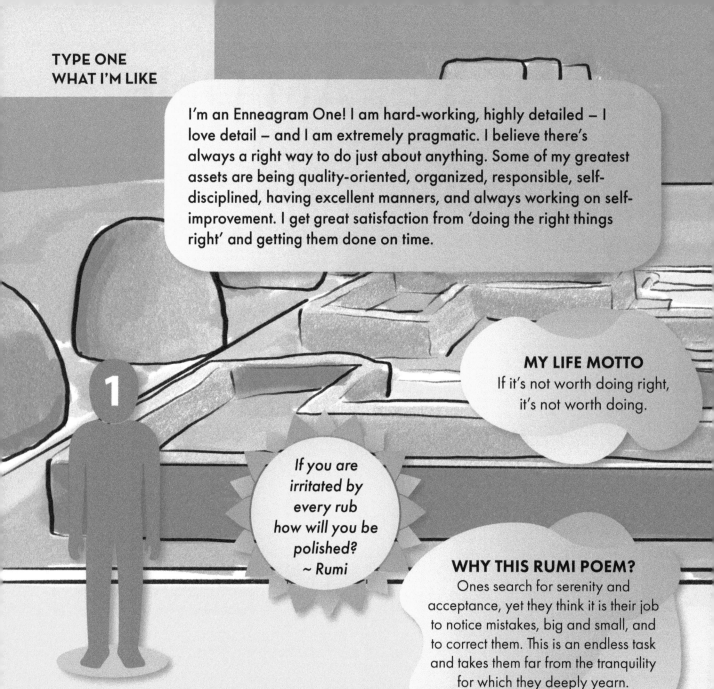

I'm an Enneagram One! I am hard-working, highly detailed – I love detail – and I am extremely pragmatic. I believe there's always a right way to do just about anything. Some of my greatest assets are being quality-oriented, organized, responsible, self-disciplined, having excellent manners, and always working on self-improvement. I get great satisfaction from 'doing the right things right' and getting them done on time.

MY LIFE MOTTO
If it's not worth doing right, it's not worth doing.

If you are irritated by every rub how will you be polished?
~ Rumi

WHY THIS RUMI POEM?
Ones search for serenity and acceptance, yet they think it is their job to notice mistakes, big and small, and to correct them. This is an endless task and takes them far from the tranquility for which they deeply yearn.

WHAT I LIKE

Conscientiousness, responsibility, excellence, honesty, timeliness, precision, polite behavior, high standards, high quality, self-control, structure and thoroughness

WHAT I DISLIKE

Laziness, lateness, dishonesty, lack of integrity or having no moral compass, not following the rules, not being responsible, bad manners, errors and mistakes

I get especially upset when I make mistakes or others make errors.

I SEARCH FOR PERFECTION

I AVOID MAKING MISTAKES

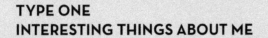

FAVORITE SONGS

"Perfect" ~ Ed Sheeran

"Maybe You're Right"
~ Miley Cyrus"

"Get It Right the First Time"
~ Billy Joel

FAVORITE SPORT | TENNIS

A game of precision and practice; when the ball hits the racket's 'sweet spot,' it's pure perfection.

MY MUSICAL INSTRUMENT | PIANO

Like an upright piano, I can be perfectly balanced, an instrument with a solid body of wood, plus ivory and metal. With both hard and smooth edges, my beautiful sound becomes an elegant addition to any classical masterpiece.

FAVORITE ACRONYMS

SMH | shaking my head

IMO | in my opinion

IKR | I know, right?

WHAT IS EASY FOR ME

Being organized, knowing how to create structure, getting things done, fixing problems, sharing opinions, being active, and being discerning – knowing when something is done well and when it is not

WHAT IS HARD FOR ME

Not showing my disapproval, not being self-critical or critical of others, accepting my mistakes, not being in control, being flexible and accepting my anger

Although I am critical of others, I am ten times harder on myself.

MY ESSENTIAL OIL | TEA TREE

Versatile, cleansing, and practical, not too sweet or sharp, just right

TEA TREE
OIL

"It's hard to be a diamond in a rhinestone world."

~ Dolly Parton

5

VERBAL CUES
» Repeated use of judging words:
   ought, should, right, wrong, must
» Offer opinions frequently
» Use precise language

NONVERBAL CUES
» Tight jaws from withholding anger
» Self-controlled bodies
» Upright posture

MORE ABOUT HOW I COMMUNICATE
» I think of myself as direct and honest, while
   also being respectful of others.
» I react very quickly to others; this can be an
   asset and a liability.
» I prefer to discuss ideas and tasks more
   than feelings and emotions.
» Others say I can be overly detailed or
   sound picky.
» People say they can sense when I'm
   upset even if I don't say anything.

"Imperfections are not inadequacies;
they are reminders that we're all
in this together."

~ Brené Brown

HOW I BEHAVE WHEN ANGRY

» Use curt or sharp statements
» Show my displeasure non-verbally through facial expressions and backward body movements
» May say nothing, even acting polite to the other person with whom I am upset
» Might make accusations related to other issues
» May become self-critical and remorseful for having expressed intense anger

MY HOT BUTTONS

» Mistakes and errors that I make
» Mistakes and errors that others make
» Another's lack of follow-through
» Feeling criticized
» Another's non-collaborative change of plans
» Feeling deceived

HOW I AM WITH CONFLICT

I don't like conflict but if it occurs, I prefer a structured, problem-solving approach that fixes the root of the problem and the issues involved.

HOW I BEHAVE WHEN STRESSED

» More easily irritated
» Short-tempered with others
» Muscles become tense
» Breathe faster and less deeply
» Can blow a fuse, becoming deeply angry
» Say things I wish I had not said

MY STRESSORS

» Making mistakes especially by me, but also by others
» Having too much to do in too short a time period
» Feeling criticized by others
» Being highly self-critical
» Others not being on time or being prepared
» Structure or processes for doing things not sufficiently clear
» Feeling under-prepared myself
» Situations feeling out of my control

ANGER is my underlying emotional state, but I don't like to acknowledge that I am angry. I don't have a lot to say about anger because I rarely, if ever, use the word. I don't like to think of myself as angry. Instead, I say that I am frustrated, upset, irritated or resentful. Sometimes I'll use the word annoyed, disappointed or displeased. I think it is impolite for people to show their anger, plus 'good' people like me don't get angry!

HOW I DEAL WITH MY ANGER

I suppress my anger, holding it in so I don't recognize how angry I really am. Sometimes I act the exact opposite of what I really feel, especially with anger, but also with anxiety or fear and sadness. I also deal with my anger through perfectionism. The more perfect something or someone is, the less I have to be angry about!

ONE HAIKU

Seeking perfection

On time focused organized

Strive for quality

3 WAYS OF DEALING WITH ANGER THROUGH PREFECTIONISM

Which version or combination am I?

3 SUBTYPES OF ENNEAGRAM ONE

Each version or subtype of One deals with anger and prefectionism in a different way

WORRY | SELF-PRESERVATION SUBTYPE

Worrying in advance and making sure every detail is perfect so I don't get angry due to mistakes

NON-ADAPTABILITY | SOCIAL SUBTYPE

Believing I am and continuously strive to be the perfect role model for others to emulate, while also trying to perfect groups and social systems as an outlet for my anger

ZEAL | ONE-TO-ONE SUBTYPE

Passionately trying to make my significant others more perfect so I don't feel angry with them

9

MY AFFIRMATION
"I AM GOOD"

Breathe so that this affirmation goes beyond just thought; allow your heart and whole body to experience this affirmation.

MY ANIMAL | ZEBRA

Practical, sturdy and grounded, I am a reminder to maintain balance in your life, no matter how busy you are. I also represent the importance of both community and individuality. My intuition is keen, and I often have a felt-sense that something that is going to happen before it even occurs. Black and white is central to me; my stripes appear black and white, and I also see in black and white. This means that while I can see clearly, I need to remember that not everything is black and white, right and wrong, good or bad.

MY COLOR | PINK

PINK represents sweet innocence and goodness, complete relaxation and childlike acceptance of what is.

Reflect on the color pink.

FRUIT OF MY ESSENCE | GRANADILLA

Crack open the hard shell on this beautiful orange orb, and you'll find a floral sweetness that is especially good mixed into juices and cocktails. Crack open a One's exterior, and you'll find the playful flow of subtle honey, unqualified transparency and pure acceptance.

CULTIVATE CALMNESS

Have you ever felt calm? Remember that moment and re-experience it in your imagination so much so that your entire body senses that experience once again. Do this every day to cultivate calmness.

ACCEPT WHAT IS

Think of something that is absolutely perfect just as it is, even though some parts of it may not be. But the whole is perfect. Think of a perfect rose, then notice that each petal may not be perfectly formed. Yet, the rose is still perfect. Find a flower, a person or a place that is perfect in this way – perfect even with its imperfections. Reflect on this, draw it, imagine it in your mind.

BECOME MORE SPONTANEOUS

Give yourself a specific amount of time each day – even if it is 10 minutes – dedicated to spontaneity. During this time, do whatever you feel like, engage in whatever captures your imagination, and suspend judgment while you do this. Simply experience and enjoy. As you become more comfortable being spontaneous, gradually add more time each day and also add new things to do.

1

"I'm 1st generation in a family of immigrants, with parents who wanted the best for me, which was, in their eyes, to become a doctor. I've always been more interested in doing the right thing, being of upstanding character, and working on self-improvement. I could be a stick-to-the-rules kind of person, but what has opened me up to be more flexible and heartfelt is my older brother, who has severe disabilities. In caring for him, out of love and not from responsibility, my heart has opened, and he has helped me realize we are all perfect in our own way."

1

Everyone and everything is perfect as it is

I experience serenity in all that occurs

ENNEAGRAM TWO

THE LOVING PERSON

I'm an Enneagram Two! I am friendly, warm, people-oriented, responsive, thoughtful, helpful, nurturing, generous and compassionate. I try very hard to put others first and not think about myself because it is important that other people know they can count on me in times of need. Some of my greatest assets are being extremely in tune with other people and being intuitive, and I love giving unexpected presents to others so they know that I care.

2

*Love yourself completely
Return to the root of your own soul
~ Rumi*

MY LIFE MOTTO
The world would be a much better place if everyone would put others first.

WHY THIS RUMI POEM?
Twos are adept at showing love for others and do so continuously. However, self-love is harder because this comes from inside, and Twos focus far more on the external and how others are responding to them. Experiencing the root of one's own soul requires a deep inner journey and the ability to self-love and self-care without being concerned about the reactions of others.

WHAT I LIKE

Warm people, kindness toward others, feeling needed and important to people, reciprocity, intuiting what other people need, strong interpersonal relationships, giving advice and providing help

WHAT I DISLIKE

People who are not empathic, selfishness, insensitivity, demands that I do things for people or respond in a certain way, and not knowing where I stand with others

I get especially distraught when my relationships are troubled in any way.

I SEARCH FOR APPRECIATION AND BEING NEEDED

I AVOID FEELING UNWORTHY

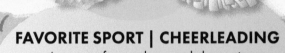

FAVORITE SONGS

"You've Got a Friend"
~ Carol King

"I Want to Talk About You"
~ John Coltrane

"I Can't Give You Anything but Love"
~ Tony Bennett & Lady Gaga

2

FAVORITE SPORT | CHEERLEADING
A sport of complete and dynamic cooperation, we are here to cheer for our team. We are fierce. We can't be beat. Go team!

FAVORITE ACRONYMS

HTH | happy to help

BFF | best friend(s) forever

RUOK | are you okay?

MY MUSICAL INSTRUMENT | HARP
Like a harp, I can pluck at your heart strings, like an angel from heaven. I'm best played next to your heart, with my angelic sounds resonating like soft bliss.

16

WHAT IS EASY FOR ME

Knowing what others want and need, being thoughtful, kind and supportive, offering useful advice, making others feel comfortable, nurturing people in a variety of ways, and sharing my resources, including my time

WHAT IS HARD FOR ME

Knowing what I feel, sensing what I need, expressing my desires, asking for help, saying 'No' to people, especially those I care about, and getting deeply angry

When relationships go awry in any way, I always ask myself "What did I do wrong?" and "How can I repair this?"

MY ESSENTIAL OIL | ROSE

Uplifting, soft sweet mood elevator easing pain and depressive symptoms

ROSE OIL

"I'm not happy all the time, and I wouldn't want to be that way because that would make me a shallow person. But I do try to find the good in everybody."

~ Dolly Parton

2

VERBAL CUES
» Ask frequent questions of others
» Soft voice unless angry
» Give compliments

MORE ABOUT HOW I COMMUNICATE
» I establish relationship easily and am generally interested in what others say.
» I'm easy to talk to and offer practical, yet insightful, suggestions and advice.
» I don't talk about myself that much except with close friends.
» If I don't like what someone is saying, I disengage from them even if they don't know it.
» I have trouble accessing the depth and details of my emotions because I want to be so positive; this gets in my way of emotional expression.

NONVERBAL CUES
» Shoulders rounded with slightly caved chests
» Eyes make warm interpersonal contact
» Smile as an invitation to engage

"Daring to set boundaries is about having the courage to love ourselves even when we risk disappointing others."

~ Brené Brown

HOW I BEHAVE WHEN ANGRY

» Keep angry feelings to myself, sometimes for long periods of time
» Think through what I'll will say in advance if I can
» Can be intensely emotional when I do say something
» May spontaneously erupt with a strongly negative remark if I've been holding it in
» Sometimes become furious, although my rage can be deeply repressed

MY HOT BUTTONS

» Feeling taken for granted
» Being taken advantage of
» Not being appreciated or valued
» Feeling unheard, unseen or discounted
» Seeing others being abused
» Being accused of having negative intentions

HOW I AM WITH CONFLICT

I don't like conflict because I worry it will harm my relationships. However, I can engage with it and then want to get all the issues and emotions surfaced for discussion. I am often surprised when someone is angry with me because I try so hard to act in ways that don't offend anyone.

HOW I BEHAVE WHEN STRESSED

» Become sleep-deprived
» Feel anxious and insecure
» Become highly self-deprecating
» Feel deeply disheartened

MY STRESSORS

» Letting others down
» Others disappointing me
» People I care about appearing angry or distant
» Others acting rudely
» Feeling ignored or taken for granted
» Not having enough sleep or relaxation
» Not being able to change an interpersonal issue that matters
» Feeling falsely accused of a wrongdoing

SORROW is my underlying emotional state, although I experience my sadness primarily in relation to other peoples' suffering, which keeps me from having to experience my own suffering. My deeper sadness is from the image I create of being a kind, generous and thoughtful person who is here to take care of others' needs. But then I feel sad if people don't perceive me this way or sad because people don't often see the true, deeper me behind the image. In addition, I become extremely hurt when I feel taken for granted given I do so much for others, but also when others do not reciprocate and offer to support me.

HOW I DEAL WITH MY SORROW

I repress my own inner sadness, keeping it down so I can focus on other people and how to help them and be important to them. This makes me feel above others because I convince myself I have no real needs. But my focus on others and their reactions to me actually makes me dependent on them. In doing so, my self-worth becomes heightened and inflated when they respond affirmatively, but deflated when they do not. In times of deflation, I feel deeply unworthy and shameful. In times of inflation, I feel especially good about myself.

TWO HAIKU

Always generous

With a need to be needed

Providing support

20

2

3 WAYS OF DEALING WITH MY SORROW THROUGH SELF-INFLATION & SELF-DEFLATION

Which version or combination am I?

3 SUBTYPES OF ENNEAGRAM TWO

Each version or subtype of Two deals with sorrow and self-inflation and self-deflation in a different way

ME FIRST/PRIVILEGE | SELF-PRESERVATION SUBTYPE

Appearing as if I need your protection by acting in a beguiling childlike way and in exchange, I will also take care of you; the prince or princess

AMBITION | SOCIAL SUBTYPE

Focusing on helping and supporting groups as a way of having a significant role in them and as a way to increase my feelings of self-worth; the emperor or empress

AGGRESSION/SEDUCTION | ONE-TO-ONE SUBTYPE

Meeting the needs of significant and important people as a way to increase my self-worth and to get my needs met by these important others; the king or queen

21

MY AFFIRMATION
"I AM LOVED"

Breathe so that this affirmation goes beyond just thought; allow your heart and whole body to experience this affirmation.

MY ANIMAL | ELEPHANT

Elephants symbolize wisdom, gentleness, and spiritual understanding and are highly sensitive and emotional. They cry, laugh, and show anger, and if a baby elephant is distressed, the entire elephant family moves to caress and soothe it, often with their trunks, which are finely tuned. Elephants do get underestimated in terms of both their power and intelligence. Looking like gentle giants, they can and will crush the world's most dangerous animals; they are highly intelligent with brains that are similar in terms of structure and complexity to the human brain and larger than those of any other land animal. Remember to honor your personal power and intellectual capabilities!

MY COLOR | GOLD

GOLD represents melting, merging, and surrendering to closeness with others.

Reflect on the color gold.

FRUIT OF MY ESSENCE | MORA

With a mix of deep purple and flashes of raspberry red, I can be sweet when diluted with water or milk and spiked with sugar, or I can add heightened flavor to certain dishes like meat and cheese. Thus, like a Two, I can be sweet or I can be spicy, depending on the situation. I can remember that I am delicious either way, making any dish even more delectable and relationships with others worth savoring as long as I am whole and ripe.

TAKE MORE CARE OF YOURSELF

Think of this as self-love; it is not selfishness. Explore what feels nurturing to you, and allow yourself to give that to yourself. Eat the food you really like. Do the things that give you pleasure. You can still offer to help others but don't drop everything on your plate in order to support them. And before you automatically say 'yes' to something or someone, ask yourself why you are saying 'yes' and if you really want to do that. If you don't, learn to say 'no' without guilt.

EXPLORE YOUR FEELINGS IN DEPTH

Ask yourself at least six times per day, "What am I feeling right now?" Each time you ask this question, explore the answer for at least five minutes. In addition, if you have a mild to moderate emotional reaction to anything, ask yourself the very same question and spend at least five minutes exploring the answer. When you get more in touch with your deeper feelings, you'll also get more connected to your real needs.

BASE YOUR SELF-WORTH ON HOW YOU FEEL ABOUT YOURSELF

This sounds really hard, but here's an easy way to practice this. Pay attention to your chest area when something goes really well – for example, someone likes you, someone has followed your advice and it worked, or you made a contribution that mattered – and notice how your chest area gets bigger or inflates. Also pay attention to your chest area when the opposite occurs – something didn't go well – and how your chest deflates. After you become aware of this, every time your chest inflates, manage the inflation so it is not as big or extended. Once you learn to not inflate as much, the deflation effect will not occur as often.

2

"This may sound strange, but I had a big issue with the check-out person at the small local market near where I live. I don't know this person at all, but whenever I go through the check-out line, I always go through this person's line. It's not because I like them, but because they never smile at me or even acknowledge that I am there. For months, I tried to get a response, but no! Although I could have gone to another check-out line, I couldn't, but why? I realized I had this deep need to get this person to like me, and this wasn't working. After some soul searching, I realized this was my issue and that I needed to go through the checkout line and really not care whether I got a response. Once I could do this – it took me nearly a month – a miracle happened. Once I stopped trying, the person actually 'saw' me. And I felt like I had been through years of therapy!"

Accessing and honoring my needs leads to freedom

I accept and value myself independent of the reactions of others

ENNEAGRAM THREE

THE EFFECTIVE PERSON

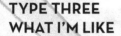

I'm an Enneagram Three! I am productive, focused, goal-oriented, confident, and results-driven. With my 'can-do' attitude, I try to be professional in everything I do, and it is very important to me that I feel and others perceive me as highly competent and able to get things done. I prefer tasks and activities rather than spending a lot of time on the emotional aspects of relationships, but people are important to me and I'm told that I read an audience well. This does not mean I don't value or feel emotions; I do. I just don't want them to get in the way of my work. This means I can adjust how I come across to achieve the impact I most want.

3

Let the beauty of what you love be what you do.
~ Rumi

MY LIFE MOTTO
Set goals, create doable plans, and everything else generally falls into place.

WHY THIS RUMI POEM?
Threes pursue what they think will get results and help them feel successful and effective in the eyes of others. To this end, they take stock of their social context, assess what a successful person would be like, act like, and decide what they should pursue to gain respect. As way to avoid failure, Threes do not pursue areas of interest that they might enjoy but may not be very good at doing. This poem is about following your own heart's desire.

WHAT I LIKE
Setting and accomplishing specific plans and goals, getting results, stimulating competitions, doing what I'm good at, knowing what's expected, achievement, success, and being respected

WHAT I DISLIKE
Wasting time, sitting still, being around incompetent people, doing nothing, focusing on my emotions at length, and feelings of real or potential failure

I become anxious at the thought that I might fail at even the smallest task, but I work hard not to show my nervousness to others.

I SEARCH FOR RESPECT AND ADMIRATION

I AVOID FAILURE

FAVORITE SONGS

"You're So Vain"
~ Carly Simon

"We Are the Champions"
~ Queen

"Ain't No Mountain High Enough"
~ Marvin Gaye, Tammi Terrell

FAVORITE SPORT | BASKETBALL

A fast-paced game where the competition is fierce and the scoring system allows for an extremely high number of points. A nice 3 pointer never hurts.

FAVORITE ACRONYMS

FTW | for the win

WFM | works for me

WTG | way to go

MY MUSICAL INSTRUMENT | ELECTRIC GUITAR

Like an electric guitar, I can be flashy and get your attention quickly, especially with my six strings attached to an amp. Nothing beats the smooth sound of a lead guitarist.

WHAT IS EASY FOR ME

Getting results, planning my day, solving problems efficiently, being personable, looking confident even when feeling sad or anxious, knowing how to get things done, being entrepreneurial, and being able to look good in a public setting

WHAT IS HARD FOR ME

Feeling unproductive, being without goals and plans, someone else arbitrarily changing my goals, trying new things that I may not be good at, talking about my emotions in depth, and being patient

Being still, to me, means being idle and lazy. How do I 'do' being still?

MY ESSENTIAL OIL | LEMON

Tangy and zestful, helps with alertness, boosting brain power and concentration

LEMON OIL

'Figure out who you are. And do it on purpose.'

~ **Dolly Parton**

TYPE THREE
HOW I COMMUNICATE AND REACT

VERBAL CUES
» Want to get to the point quickly
» Logical, clear, concise speech
» Give ideas in sets of 3 points

NONVERBAL CUES
» Shoulders more horizontal than rounded
» Energy in face and upper body
» Confident demeanor

MORE ABOUT HOW I COMMUNICATE
» I am quick on my feet, typically acting with poise and confidence when speaking in public.
» I like to get to the point quickly and expect others to do the same.
» I look around regularly to check out how others are reacting to me or what I'm saying.
» I don't like to discuss topics I know little about or get into areas that might reflect negatively on me.
» My social skills are well developed, although I get quite impatient with lengthy discussions; then I can be abrupt.

3

"Authenticity is the daily practice of letting go of who we think we're supposed to be and embracing who we are."

~ Brené Brown

HOW I BEHAVE WHEN ANGRY

» Unlikely to say I am upset until my anger builds
» My body language is unlikely to give strong clues about my feelings
» Ask a short sequence of structured, pointed questions as a way to make my point
» Can use a sharp tone of voice with clipped sentences to express myself

MY HOT BUTTONS

» Being in a position of potential failure
» Not looking good personally or professionally
» Being blamed for the poor performance or behavior of others
» Working with less than competent people
» Not receiving credit for what I have done
» Having to discuss emotional issues at length

HOW I AM WITH CONFLICT

I don't particularly like conflict, but I will deal with it when I have to do so. My preferred approach is a non-emotional, rational problem-solving approach; then I want to be done with it!

HOW I BEHAVE WHEN STRESSED

» Even more of a workaholic and hyper-driven than normal
» Abrupt and irritable
» Highly anxious and verbally aggressive
» Deeply angry and sometimes hostile
» Lethargic and isolated from others who can give me support and feedback

MY STRESSORS

» Believing failure is possible or looming
» Having my self-confidence or sense of competence challenged
» Thinking I may lose something or someone I deeply wanted
» When I have strong feelings
» When I feel demands to discuss emotional issues at length
» Having no specific goals to pursue
» Having my plans thwarted for any reason

SORROW is my underlying emotional state, although I don't let myself feel it very often, as feeling sad keeps me from feeling and appearing confident and competent. My sadness comes from my belief that I am not valuable for who I am, but only of value for what I can accomplish. Even more, I have to keep proving myself, or so I believe, which can be very tiring and often disheartening. I have to keep aiming for the next big accomplishment, making sure I don't fail. And because my sense of value is so dependent on what I do, I am not really sure who I am beneath my successful and effective exterior.

HOW I DEAL WITH MY SORROW

I push my sadness to the side so I don't have to deal with this feeling and can keep moving forward with goals and plans, tasks and activities. Keeping active and achieving results makes me feel productive and accomplished and keeps me away from emotions that might derail my sense of value. I believe that 'I am what I do,' but also identify with roles – the good student, the effective worker, the best boss, the ideal son or parent, the accomplished athlete – and activities such as running, yoga and cycling. I also identify with the positive image I've created and don't like to acknowledge or show aspects of myself that do not conform to that image.

THREE HAIKU

Making things happen

Endlessly creating plans

A thirst for success

32

3 WAYS OF DEALING WITH MY SORROW BY CREATING AN IDEALIZED IMAGE OF SUCCESS

Which version or combination am I?

3 SUBTYPES OF ENNEAGRAM THREE

Each version or subtype of Three deals with sorrow and image in a different way

SECURITY | SELF-PRESERVATION SUBTYPE

Create an image of a good or ideal person who is self-reliant, independent and hardworking with an image of having no image

PRESTIGE | SOCIAL SUBTYPE

Create an image of being highly successful and admirable, liking to be around other successful people to reinforce my own status

MASCULINITY/FEMININITY | ONE-TO-ONE SUBTYPE

Create an image of being a highly attractive male or female to attract significant others to me, and then support that person's success

33

MY AFFIRMATION "I AM VALUABLE"

Breathe so that this affirmation goes beyond just thought; allow your heart and whole body to experience this affirmation.

MY ANIMAL | PEACOCK

The peacock represents rebirth and reinvention, knowing it's never too late to change course. In addition, the peacock means it's time to look at things differently. See the beauty of what is inside – not the beautiful feathers or how the peacock behaves – and experience the value of what is intrinsic rather than external. With deep confidence and intrinsic self-respect, the peacock reminds you to both own your truth and stay true to yourself. Peacocks also represent the ability to access your dreams; just make sure they are your dreams, what you deeply want, not what you think you should want.

MY COLOR | PEARL

PEARL represents autonomy, identity, going beyond activity into a greater sense of being.

Reflect on the color pearl.

FRUIT OF MY ESSENCE | GUAYABA

From the outside, the guayaba can be mistaken for a small green pear. Inside, the shock of hot-pink flesh is unmistakably wonderful. Like a guayaba, Threes can identify as another fruit, in this case a pear. No need to be a pear when you're a guayaba; your inner fruit is delicious and beloved.

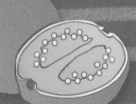

BE STILL, EVEN WHEN YOU'RE DOING SOMETHING

Being still is difficult for just about everyone, so it's not just you. And because you are a person used to moving and action, you can learn to be doing something from a place of stillness. Here are some examples. When you are eating, don't 'eat on the run.' Sit down or stand up, but stay present to the eating experience. Taste every morsel and savor the experience. When you are reading, read every word and enjoy the experience of reading, paying attention to every word and concept, rather than reading with a goal in mind. Experience and savor the reading process. Be in the present moment whatever you are doing: taking a walk, grocery shopping, feeding the dog or cat, and more.

REFLECT ON YOUR HEART'S DESIRE

The question to ask yourself is "What is my heart's desire? What do I truly want?" You may have never asked yourself this before, so embrace what emerges in response, even if there is no answer. But if you do have an answer, ask yourself this: "Do I want this because I think I should, or is this what I truly want?"

ASK YOURSELF, "WHO AM I?"

This question is about who you really are, in addition to or at a deeper level, than a listing of roles, functions and activities in which you engage. You can feel proud of your accomplishments and also recognize that who you are is more than that, deeper than that. Try completing this sentence multiple times: "I am...." Explore personal qualities – for example, kind, insightful, encouraging – and things you love – for example, a lover of animals, a person who enjoys good food. There are no right or wrong answers. There are simply answers. Do the above activity daily, even writing down your responses.

"Although I have always been productive and accomplished, an event happened that shook my comfortable world. Driving to work — I go the same route every day because it is efficient and effective — I noticed something on the side of the street where I live: a plant that flowers all year long with one beautiful flower. I'd never noticed this before. I stopped my car and just took in the beauty of this flower, for how long, I don't know. Back in my car, I started noticing things along the way I'd never seen before and began to wonder what else in my life I was not paying full attention to. Immediately, I thought of my four-year-old son and realized that I'm not fully present to him when we are together. That realization rattled me, and I then committed to being fully present to him. This has changed everything. I am still as productive as ever, probably even more so. My blinders have come off, and I now see what is actually there around me."

I am valued for who I really am

I now know the difference between 'being' and 'doing'

ENNEAGRAM FOUR

THE ORIGINAL PERSON

TYPE FOUR
WHAT I'M LIKE

I'm an Enneagram Four! Let me explain what I am like, with the hope that I can express myself so you can understand me, which is very important to me! For my whole life, I've been on a journey to figure out who I am and why I have always felt different from other people. I am a deep person, highly introspective, and interested in the world of feelings, the meaning of life and creative self-expression. It is important to me that I feel unique and special. My intuitive abilities are quite strong, and I am sensitive and compassionate.

4

You are not a drop in the ocean. You are the entire ocean in a single drop.
~ Rumi

MY LIFE MOTTO
Look for the universal in the particular, the joy in the pain, and find what makes you uniquely you.

WHY THIS RUMI POEM?
Fours are continuously searching for deeper, profound and unending experience and connections, and when this does not occur – for example, being out of real contact with themselves or feeling separated from others – they become distressed, sad, or angry. Part of this is based on their feeling of being insignificant, not-enough, or deficient. This poem illuminates that which is more true, if only they knew it.

WHAT I LIKE
Creativity, exploring emotions, deep conversations, feeling inspired, feeling connected to myself and others, authentic interactions with other people, self-expression, symbolism and feeling understood

WHAT I DISLIKE
Adhering to social convention, feeling bored or stagnant, insincerity, inauthentic people, shallowness, conformism, feeling rejected, and tastelessness in any form

I am extremely sensitive in general, and particularly so to feeling either rejected or deficient.

I SEARCH FOR DEEP CONNECTIONS AND EMOTIONAL EXPRESSION

I AVOID FEELING REJECTED OR NOT-GOOD-ENOUGH

39

FAVORITE SPORT | OUTHOUSE RACING

Two pushers, two pullers, one rider and one outhouse; that's the team. The outhouse is mounted on skis – must be done on an icy street – plus one toilet seat and a toilet paper dispenser also required. Pretty unique, no?

FAVORITE SONGS

"Yesterday"
~ The Beatles

"Bohemian Rhapsody"
~ Queen

"Will You Still Love Me Tomorrow"
~ Carole King

FAVORITE ACRONYMS

VSF | very sad face

WDYMBT | what did you mean by that

FOMO | fear of missing out

4

MY MUSICAL INSTRUMENT | CELLO

Like this most resonant of instruments, I am deeply connected, at one with my instrument when I play. Imagine the famous cellist Yo Yo Ma. So evocative am I, you can see me in paintings by Picasso and Van Gogh, deeply strong and beautiful.

40

WHAT IS EASY FOR ME

Being creative, listening to others with compassion, inspiring myself and others, going deeply into my own inner experience, expressing myself through some artistic or symbolic form, and being emotionally attuned

WHAT IS HARD FOR ME

Accepting criticism, staying in the present moment, not taking things personally, expressing myself exactly as I feel and experience, and not comparing myself to others

I compare myself to others constantly and didn't realize this immediately because I thought everyone else did this too.

MY ESSENTIAL OIL | JASMINE

Derived from delicate white flowers, a beautiful, romantic essence used through the centuries

JASMINE OIL

"The way I see it, if you want a rainbow, you gottta' put up with the rain."

~ **Dolly Parton**

VERBAL CUES
» Frequent sharing of personal stories
» Frequent use of me, my, mine, and I
» Deliberate word choice

NONVERBAL CUES
» Appear focused inward
» Wet or moist eyes
» Intense

MORE ABOUT HOW I COMMUNICATE
» I really like real conversations, meaningful topics and deep feelings expressed; otherwise, I disengage.
» I can go really deep with people, listening and sharing for as long as it takes.
» My word choice is often deliberate because I want to make sure my words reflect my truest thoughts and inner experiences.
» I really enjoy sharing my own personal experiences and stories with other people.
» People say I am intense in my interactions; it's not my intention to be intense, but I do come across that way.

4

"Because true belonging only happens when we present our authentic, imperfect selves to the world, our sense of belonging can never be greater than our level of self-acceptance."

~ Brené Brown

HOW I BEHAVE WHEN ANGRY

» Experience multiple feelings simultaneously and intensely
» Excessively analyze the situation in order to understand
» May say something in an extremely blunt way
» Sometimes have a delayed reaction
» Can become extremely quiet
» Hold on to and replay my feelings for long periods of time

MY HOT BUTTONS

» Feeling ignored or slighted
» Feeling misunderstood
» Feeling cut off when I am expressing myself
» Being asked to do something contrary to my values
» Anything that elicits a feeling in me of not being good enough

HOW I AM WITH CONFLICT

I am extremely sensitive to feeling not good enough or rejected in any way; it feels like a dagger in my heart and I can become withdrawn, deeply sad or very angry and even explosive.

HOW I BEHAVE WHEN STRESSED

» Moody
» Self-reflective and very quiet
» Self-blaming
» Depressed and/or agitated
» Accusatory toward others
» Aggressively angry
» Highly emotional

MY STRESSORS

» Feeling slighted, unacknowledged, or rejected in any way
» Feeling blamed or accused
» Others interrupting or cutting me off verbally or non-verbally so I can't express myself adequately or completely
» Others misunderstanding or misinterpreting my ideas, feelings, actions or intentions
» Not fully understanding my own reactions and then having difficulty expressing myself clearly
» Comparing myself to others and then perceiving myself as deficient

SORROW is my underlying emotional state, and I am very familiar with the state of melancholy, which feels wistful and not necessarily like a bad thing. Melancholy keeps me in touch with my inner self and with humanity at large. It can also inspire my self-expression in a variety of forms. My sadness comes from my sensitivity to universal human suffering, but also from my belief that I am different from other people and that I suffer more than they do. I keep trying to discover the source of why I feel this way. I compare myself to other people in small and big ways to find the answer. Am I different and defective? Am I different and superior? Am I just different? I just don't know the answer.

HOW I DEAL WITH MY SORROW

I value emotions, even if I am not always comfortable with them, and believe 'I am what I feel.' My melancholic responses, plus the noticing of my deficiencies, help me feel connected to myself and the universal human condition. I internalize negative responses from others – including perceived negative reactions even if these may not be the case – and this gives me a vast reservoir of sadness and suffering.

FOUR HAIKU

Seeks deep connection

Pushed and pulled by emotion

Individual

44

3 WAYS OF DEALING WITH MY SORROW THROUGH MY RELATIONSHIP TO SUFFERING

Which version or combination am I?

3 SUBTYPES OF ENNEAGRAM FOUR

Each version or subtype of Four deals with sorrow and suffering in a different way

RECKLESS/DAUNTLESS | SELF-PRESERVATION SUBTYPE

Suffering in silence by being stoic and highly active, even doing some risky things to stay more upbeat; suffering without complaining and I want you to notice

SHAME | SOCIAL SUBTYPE

Suffering openly and focusing more on my deficiencies; joining groups but also feeling marginal to them, like I don't really belong; suffering more openly and I want you to notice

COMPETITION | ONE-TO-ONE SUBTYPE

Suffering intensely, then expressing my needs outwardly and also being highly competitive as a way to gain your attention and be acknowledged

45

MY AFFIRMATION
"I BELONG"

Breathe so that this affirmation
goes beyond just thought; allow
your heart and whole body to
experience this affirmation.

MY ANIMAL | TIGER

The tiger represents raw feelings and emotions,
both willpower and courage, and particularly the
personal strength to ride the rough waves of life
with energy and passion. The tiger also provides
the ability to deflect anger or aggression that
is directed at you, helping you deal with strong
emotions effectively, whether they are yours
or those of others. Highly intuitive, tigers are
especially adept at following their instincts.

MY COLOR | RAINBOW

RAINBOW represents simple, direct
experience of ourselves in our entirety,
our truest self.

Reflect on the rainbow with its
many colors.

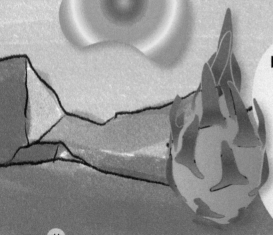

FRUIT OF MY ESSENCE | DRAGON FRUIT

With red and green coloration, the dragon fruit's
appearance is both dramatic and beautiful, with
a flavor that is surprisingly subtle. While Fours can
appear vivid and striking, the most delicious part
of a dragon fruit lies in the inner white fruit with
its intricate black seeds. What lies within Fours,
underneath the intense feelings, is a deeper self
with true constancy and balance.

APPRECIATE WHAT IS HAPPENING NOW

As you engage in everyday activities and tasks, some of which may normally seem ordinary, boring or tedious, bring yourself into the present moment instead of remembering the past or dreaming about or anticipating the future. How you do this is to savor each moment of the activity or task. If you are slicing a tomato, feel the knife in your hand, the texture of the tomato under your fingers, and the process of slicing through the tomato's variations in texture. If you are on your cell phone, feel your fingers touching the phone, notice the way your mind works as it decides what to press on the phone and your somatic reaction to what appears on screen. These are examples of being able to "appreciate what is happening now."

REFLECT ON HOW YOU COMPARE YOURSELF TO OTHERS

Although everyone compares themselves to others as part of being human, Fours do so continuously as a way to find out why they feel different from or less than others. The questions to reflect on are these: *How does this constant comparing work? What factors tend to elicit this response in me? What alternative behavior would better support me in my self-acceptance and self-development?*

CREATE EFFECTIVE FILTERS FOR NEGATIVITY COMING FROM THE OUTSIDE

Simply put, Fours tend to absorb and internalize negative information about themselves – perceived or actual information – without sorting whether it is true or useful. This creates an abundance of negativity about self. With positive information, Fours deflect it, so it does not get internally processed. The key is to set up effective filters that can be used at the moment when negative or positive information presents itself. These creative filters can then sort out what is not true or useful, but allow in data that is true and useful. You can get creative here: dimmer switches, uniquely decorated screens, imaginary guardians that know what to let in and what to not, just as examples. Let your filters work on your behalf. Setting up effective filters can change everything!

"My whole life, I wondered why I felt so different from other people, especially because I have a twin. We are not like each other at all; he is like other people, but I am not. I actually see musical notes, but I see them as colors. The color resonates with a particular tone, which is that note, which I then hear. What does it all mean? Once I realized that my "differentness" was neither a liability nor an asset and did not make me worse than or better than others, I could relax. Different is sometimes just simply different. And in some ways, being different can be a gift. I've parlayed this particular gift into becoming a musician, although I also have another vocation that pays the bills. My love of making music sustains me, and my acceptance that we are all special or different in our own ways has given me a heightened sense of belonging and connection."

Nothing is missing and we are all connected

I experience an inner state of balance and equilibrium

ENNEAGRAM FIVE

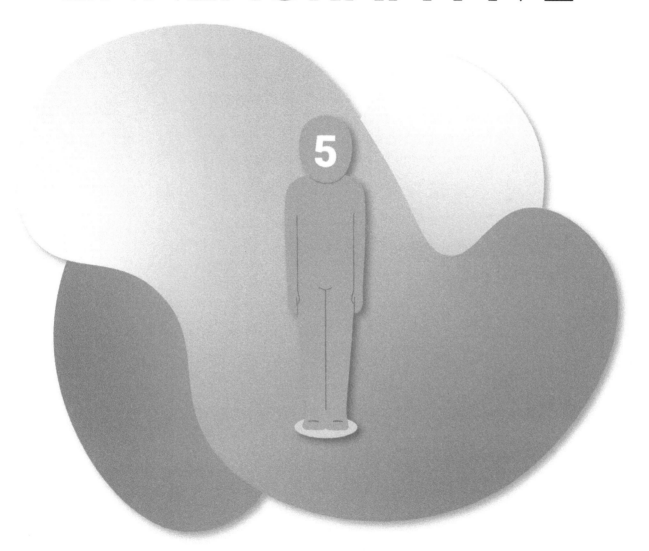

THE WISE PERSON

I'm an Enneagram Five! I'll keep this short because I don't like to talk about myself. At the same time, I think it is very important that you get accurate information about me – and Fives in general – which sometimes requires more words. As a private person, interested in life yet removed or detached from it in a sense, I like to observe rather than directly engage. People tell me I am somewhat mysterious or at least a mystery to them; that's OK with me. I like data and information so that I can understand and make sense of the world. It is also essential that I manage and conserve my time, resources and interactions; otherwise, I feel entirely depleted.

5

*Open your hands
if you want
to be held.
~ Rumi*

MY LIFE MOTTO

It's important to understand everything that matters to you; it helps you figure out how to navigate through life and keeps you interested.

WHY THIS RUMI POEM?

Fives appear as if they need very little from others and their environments; they believe resources are scarce and must be conserved and preserved. As a result, Fives become highly autonomous, relying on little outside themselves. At the same time, deep inside, Fives want fuller engagement with others and deep connection but to do so, they must be open and receptive. This is the meaning of the poem.

WHAT I LIKE
Knowledge, insight, wisdom, intellectual stimulation, competence, people who respect my physical space and boundaries, learning information in-depth, and time to myself

WHAT I DISLIKE
Surprises, demands on my time and resources, depletion of my energy, invasiveness, loss of privacy, emotionality especially when it is excessive, people not doing what they say they will do, and feeling overwhelmed

I automatically detach from my feelings in real time and have always done so, but I do experience many of them later when I am alone.

I SEARCH FOR WISDOM AND KNOWLEDGE

I AVOID INTRUSION BY OTHERS AND LOSS OF ENERGY

FAVORITE SONGS

"You Don't Know Me"
~ Ray Charles

"Private Dancer"
~ Tina Turner

"If You Could Read My Mind"
~ Gordon Lightfoot

FAVORITE SPORT | GOLF

Golf is ideal, as it can be played by oneself – ah, relaxing, private time alone – or with another person or a group. To be really good requires skill, patience and practice, and being alone in a peaceful setting allows me time to recharge my energy.

5

MY MUSICAL INSTRUMENT | FLUTE

The flute is simple and complex, silver and unassuming. My beautiful sound and spirit add to any musical composition. Although my vibrational quality may be unpretentious, when I engage with other instruments, the sound becomes other worldly. And I often play solos.

FAVORITE ACRONYMS

FYI | for your information

NOYB | none of your business

P&C | private and confidential

WHAT IS EASY FOR ME

Being cerebral, independent, objective, logical, analytical, insightful, cool in a crisis, systematic, autonomous, self-contained and giving others space

WHAT IS HARD FOR ME

Being spontaneous, engaging easily and comfortably with others in unstructured social environments, talking about feelings, small talk, experiencing my feelings in real time, and sharing personal information about myself

I can be spontaneous, but only with people I completely trust and have known for a long time. There are not many of these people in my life.

MY ESSENTIAL OIL | FRANKINCENSE

Gentle and unassuming, used by ancient civilizations for sacred, meditative practices

FRANKINCENSE
OIL

"I just don't feel like I have to explain myself."

~ **Dolly Parton**

VERBAL CUES
» Talk at length if knowledgeable
» More often quiet than talkative
» Use minimal language

NONVERBAL CUES
» Eyes appear as if observing themselves
» Self-contained body
» Low animation

MORE ABOUT HOW I COMMUNICATE
» I like to take in and absorb what is occurring before I interact with others.
» Although some people say I talk very little, I talk quite at length when I know a great deal about a topic and also feel like sharing this information with others.
» I talk much more about facts than feelings; emotional conversations, especially if prolonged, are not comfortable for me.
» People sometimes say they can't read me; well, ask without demanding, and I may tell you.
» Ask me what I feel, and I may tell you what I think, but ask me what I think, and I might tell you what I feel; I get confused between these two areas.

5

"We don't have to do all of it alone. We were never meant to."

~ Brené Brown

54

HOW I BEHAVE WHEN ANGRY

» Disconnect emotionally
» Say little
» Pull back, but may not show this outwardly
» Retain the experience mentally and process it later when alone
» May express anger directly and intensely when extremely angry

MY HOT BUTTONS

» Another breaking my confidence or privacy
» Being surprised or startled
» Dishonesty
» Unpredictable or overwhelming tasks
» Emotionally-charged situations
» Experiencing someone as invasive on a physical, verbal or psychological level

HOW I AM WITH CONFLICT

I don't like emotionally charged situations; they feel draining and unnecessary. I do get very angry when someone violates my privacy or confidential information, especially if I trusted them.

HOW I BEHAVE WHEN STRESSED

» Highly withdrawn
» Exhausted and depleted
» Brooding
» Even more emotionally detached than normal
» Angry
» Isolated
» Depressed

MY STRESSORS

» Believing someone intends to harm me
» Someone betrays my trust
» Information being withheld from me
» Interacting longer or having to be more forthcoming than I am comfortable doing
» Feeling invaded in some way
» My autonomy being compromised
» An ideal I hold dear being violated
» Feeling overwhelmed by either work or demands on my time and energy
» Demands made on me for emotional disclosure
» Someone with too much energy coming toward me

FEAR is my underlying emotional state, and I am aware of this; my fear is twofold: intrusion by others and loss of energy to such a degree that I can feel entirely drained and depleted. I have a belief system that there is not enough to go around, so I must conserve the scarce resources that I have. Privacy, space and energy are just some of the critical resources we cannot afford to squander. In addition, I am watchful and observant so as to pick up cues in the environment, including but not limited to those that have to do with other people. I don't trust many people, with the exception being those who I have known for many years and who have sustained the test of time.

HOW I DEAL WITH MY FEAR

There are three different ways. First, I withdraw so I can more easily observe in a dispassionate way. I've already disconnected from my feelings in real time which helps me be more objective and less subjective. Second, I use my mind to strategize how to prevent or minimize anything that concerns me or feels dangerous in some way. Third, I conserve or guard the relevant resources I possess so that these are not squandered. These strategies help me feel protected and minimize disruption.

FIVE HAIKU

A thirst for knowledge

Conservation space

Recluse with a book

56

3 WAYS OF DEALING WITH MY FEAR THROUGH GUARDING MYSELF AND MY RESOURCES

Which version or combination am I?

3 SUBTYPES OF ENNEAGRAM FIVE

Each version or subtype of Five deals with fear by guarding self and resources in a different way

CASTLE | SELF-PRESERVATION SUBTYPE

Making sure I do not get overextended physically, over-commit, and needing my own private space, like my castle

TOTEM | SOCIAL SUBTYPE

Connecting and sharing ideals – metaphorically, totems are symbols for ideals – with a group of people who also share my important values, while still guarding my personal privacy and energy

CONFIDENCE | ONE-TO-ONE SUBTYPE

Having a special relationship with someone who shares what is important to me and with whom I can share my confidential information and have confidence in, then guarding this very private relationship from outside forces

MY AFFIRMATION
"I AM ENOUGH"

Breathe so that this affirmation goes beyond just thought; allow your heart and whole body to experience this affirmation.

MY ANIMAL | OWL

The owl has the ability to see what others miss, perceiving the deeper meaning of things and discovering the hidden treasures in life. Owls see beyond deceit and masks, with the ability to cut through illusions. They also represent wisdom, deep connection and intuitive knowledge.

MY COLOR | DIAMOND

DIAMOND represents knowing that true wisdom comes from the complete, integrated experience of mind, heart and body.

Reflect on a diamond with its many facets.

FRUIT OF MY ESSENCE | CHERIMOYA

This greyish green fruit has a subtle appearance both inside and out, and on first glance, it is unassuming. Inside is a different story, but it is not obvious from the exterior, just like a Five. Inside, you'll find the profound simplicity of powerful seeds. And its custard-like interior flesh tastes like a combination of banana, pineapple, and bubblegum.
Let us taste what is inside.

BREATHE MORE FULLY

You may or may not realize this, but your breathing is most likely restricted to breathing into your head and neck without allowing your breath to filter down to the rest of your body. Focus on breathing more gently and rhythmically through your neck to your upper torso, heart area and stomach, and eventually, through your lower torso and legs. This won't happen immediately, but gradually you can do this, so take your time. Breathing more fully allows you more access to your body which will also give you more energy and vitality, helping you feel less depleted. It will also give you more information about yourself, such as which parts of your body feel tense and which parts feel more relaxed.

LEARN TO IDENTIFY FEELINGS THORUGH SOMATIC EXPERIENCE

Once you can breathe more deeply, this will become easier, but you can do it even before you've mastered breathing more fully. Every time you feel something in your body, whatever it is, notice it, identify the exact location if you can, and then ask this: *is this only physical or is it also associated with a feeling? If so, what am I feeling?* Remember that not every somatic experience is necessarily a feeling, but every feeling has a somatic experience associated with it. Somatic cues can help you be more emotionally agile.

ALLOW YOURSELF TO BOTH OFFER AND ACCEPT RESOURCES FROM OTHERS, HOWEVER SMALL

Your independence and autonomy are admirable and useful, yet they can also cause you to be less resourced than you need to be and less connected to other people. Learn to do this, however counter-intuitive it may feel, and you can do it in small steps. To make an offer to others, one idea is to simply offer a little more time listening to a person than you would normally do. To accept a resource from another person – for example, asking someone for an idea or referral, accepting an offer from someone for some extra time so you can share some of your thoughts – are important first steps. Start small so you can expand if you want to.

59

"This is a simple story of how small actions can have big consequences. Although I valued how autonomous and independent I've always been, when I became more in touch with my feelings, I recognized that my aloneness was also causing me to feel lonely. When I looked at my behavior, it was clear that I often didn't go to social events, and if I did, I came late, left early, and stood outside the group. No wonder I hardly interacted with anyone. I decided to experiment. I started going to social events early, stood in the middle of the gathering, and smiled at people. Interactions with others became much easier and even enjoyable in small doses that I could control. I've since joined a running club, where I can be alone, in a sense, in a group, but also enjoy some social time, if I choose, with those sharing this common interest. Lonely no more!

Only through direct engagement can all things be known

I care and am engaged and can be truly non-attached

ENNEAGRAM SIX

THE LOYAL PERSON

TYPE SIX
WHAT I'M LIKE

6

I'm an Enneagram Six! I am a complex person and, in some ways, consistently inconsistent. For example, I am risk-taking and risk averse. This makes sense because everything involves some risk, and I am very good at doing risk assessments and calculating possibilities and likely outcomes. Trusting others and trusting situations is very important to me. I am also very loyal until my loyalty to something or someone proves that it was ill-placed. Then I am no longer loyal. I am also reliable, committed, insightful, persevering, and a very good problem solver, which I enjoy. In general, groups or teams are something I am drawn to for two reasons. There is safety in groups of like-minded people, and groups of clever people can be better problem solvers than one person alone.

MY LIFE MOTTO
There are no simple solutions to life's complex problems; keep your eyes open and your humor intact.

Once the seeds of faith take root It cannot be blown away Even by the strongest wind
~ Rumi

WHY THIS RUMI POEM?
Sixes want to trust others and their environments, but fundamentally, they want to be able to trust themselves and their own inner guidance. In a world that can involve perpetual uncertainty, the faith and the conviction that they can truly trust themselves, rather than looking to the outside for this, provides Sixes the path to certitude in an ambiguous world.

WHAT I LIKE
Predictability, safety, certainty, people I can count on, thinking through issues fully, stimulating challenges, authority figures who can be trusted, feeling prepared, people who do what they say they will do, and meaning and contribution

WHAT I DISLIKE
Deception, people with hidden agendas, untrustworthy people, authority figures who misuse or abuse their power, ambiguity, simplistic thinking, and people who tell me I'm just imagining something

I doubt myself and doubt others on a regular basis, although I don't want everyone to know this about me.

I SEARCH FOR MEANING, CERTAINTY AND TRUST

I AVOID NEGATIVE SCENARIOS FROM OCCURRING

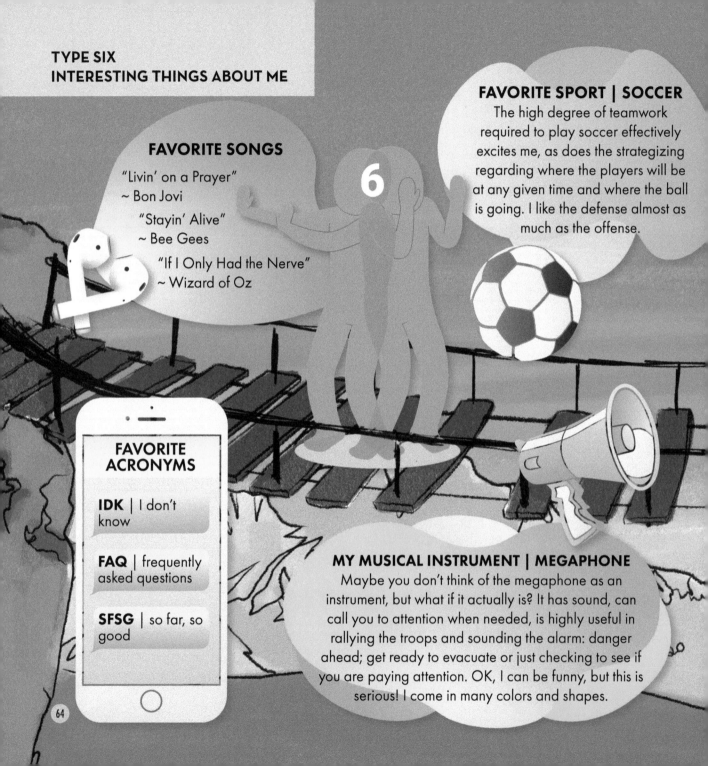

FAVORITE SONGS

"Livin' on a Prayer"
~ Bon Jovi

"Stayin' Alive"
~ Bee Gees

"If I Only Had the Nerve"
~ Wizard of Oz

FAVORITE SPORT | SOCCER

The high degree of teamwork required to play soccer effectively excites me, as does the strategizing regarding where the players will be at any given time and where the ball is going. I like the defense almost as much as the offense.

FAVORITE ACRONYMS

IDK | I don't know

FAQ | frequently asked questions

SFSG | so far, so good

MY MUSICAL INSTRUMENT | MEGAPHONE

Maybe you don't think of the megaphone as an instrument, but what if it actually is? It has sound, can call you to attention when needed, is highly useful in rallying the troops and sounding the alarm: danger ahead; get ready to evacuate or just checking to see if you are paying attention. OK, I can be funny, but this is serious! I come in many colors and shapes.

WHAT IS EASY FOR ME

Thinking, analyzing, contingency planning, being humorous about real life situations, problem solving, collaboration, being loyal, asking questions, being curious, and being prepared for various alternatives

WHAT IS HARD FOR ME

Trusting myself, knowing when I'm imagining something or when I'm being intuitive, dealing with ambiguity, trusting someone once the trust has been lost, and relaxing enough so I'm not constantly thinking

I ask a lot of 'What if' questions as a way to understand, but also as a way get others to think about situations more deeply; this can come across as pessimism, but I don't necessarily feel pessimistic.

MY ESSENTIAL OIL | MYRRH

Dynamic and versatile, kills harmful bacteria, supports health, eases digestion and insomnia

MYRRH
OIL

"You'll never do a whole lot unless you're brave enough to try."

~ Dolly Parton

65

VERBAL CUES
» Hesitant or highly assertive speech
» Frequent use of 'What if' questions
» Use analytical language

6

MORE ABOUT HOW I COMMUNICATE
» I don't like people who brag or are full of themselves.
» I'm an excellent problem solver and try to help others address issues.
» Humor is so important, not standard jokes, but the ability to laugh about life.
» I've been told people can sense when I am worried about something, which takes me by surprise.
» I know I can come across as an intense person, but I don't always experience myself that way.

"Faith is a place of mystery, where we find the courage to believe in what we cannot see and the strength to let go of our fear of uncertainty."

~ Brené Brown

NONVERBAL CUES
» Darting eyes as if scanning
» Hyper-vigilant demeanor
» Appear tense or stressed

HOW I BEHAVE WHEN ANGRY

- » May withdraw
- » Become highly emotional
- » Engage in intensive analysis
- » May be highly reactive and blurt out my reaction in ways I later regret
- » Imagine and project my own thoughts, feelings, fears, and motivations onto others, but often do not know I'm doing this

MY HOT BUTTONS

- » Pressure; I already pressure myself more than enough
- » Lack of genuineness
- » Lack of warmth
- » Being told I'm imagining something
- » Lack of commitment and loyalty
- » Abusive use of authority

HOW I AM WITH CONFLICT

I feel really uncomfortable when others are angry with me, but especially so when I am angry. Anger makes me feel unsafe, and my own anger often makes me feel guilty. I have trouble giving myself permission to get angry, although I do get angry and I know this.

HOW I BEHAVE WHEN STRESSED

- » Worry even more than normal
- » Become highly anxious
- » Fret about extremely small secondary items
- » Feel wound-up and exhausted
- » Spin in circular thinking about my worst-case scenarios
- » Self-doubt increases dramatically
- » Become highly reactive, angry and aggressive

MY STRESSORS

- » Attempting to make an important decision and being unsure of the consequences
- » An authority figure wanting to discuss something with me and not being sure what will occur
- » Breaking a rule and imagining the negative consequences
- » Perceiving, imagining or hearing that someone plans to cause me harm
- » Someone challenging an opinion I believe to be true or is related to my deeper values
- » Perceiving a situation as extremely uncertain, volatile or dangerous
- » Being under stress already, then having additional pressure put on me

FEAR is my underlying emotional state, and I know this about myself, but I would call myself more of an anticipatory planner or creative problem solver than a fearful person. If I can figure things out in advance, then no reason to fear. However, fear is still there in various forms: anxiety even if mild, concern, feeling perplexed and more. Trust is a core issue for me. I can be overly trusting and then get distraught if my trust has been misplaced. I can also be highly skeptical, testing others and situations to determine if I can and should trust. Often, I ask many 'What if' questions to make sure the ground is firm and to determine if I and others have thought through all the relevant information upon which to make a decision or act.

HOW I DEAL WITH MY FEAR

I deal with my fear in complex ways. I have a finely tuned antenna for picking up what might be happening now or in the future, and this continuously operates in me. My antenna helps me sense when someone is deceptive, untrustworthy or when a situation that seems fine may not be. Sometimes I am or act compliant so as to stay under the radar. Sometimes I act defiant and confront people or issues in a strong and forward way. I may not even know in advance which version of me will show up: compliant, defiant or both. I may take very few risks. Alternatively, I may take big risks – for example, physical ones – to feel adrenalized and prove to myself and others I am not afraid, even when I actually am. All of this is so I can feel safe.

SIX HAIKU

Complex perceptive

An antenna for danger

Trust loyalty doubt

6

3 WAYS OF DEALING WITH MY FEAR THROUGH FINDING A WAY TO FEEL SAFE

Which version or combination am I?

3 SUBTYPES OF ENNEAGRAM SIX

Each version or subtype of Six deals with fear and staying safe in a different way

WARMTH | SELF-PRESERVATION SUBTYPE

Being warm toward others and also creating and being loyal to tribes comprised of friends, peers and family because I believe there is safety in numbers; using self-doubt as a way to feel prepared and safe

DUTY | SOCIAL SUBTYPE

Knowing and following prescribed ways of behaving based on what authorities want and social groups expect, as well as doing my duty to and for the group; following the rules and staying within the boundaries as a way to feel safe

STRENGTH & BEAUTY | ONE-TO-ONE SUBTYPE

Appearing fearless and bold, charismatic or fierce as a way to prove to myself and others that I have no fear; using boldness and assertion as a way to feel safe

MY AFFIRMATION "I AM SAFE"

Breathe so that this affirmation goes beyond just thought; allow your heart and whole body to experience this affirmation.

MY ANIMAL | HAWK

The hawk has many meanings: self-awareness, truth, perspective, the power to see with clear vision. Even more, the hawk has the power to fully focus, serving as a messenger to the world, sometimes bearing important messages that others prefer not to hear. In addition, the hawk comes with the power to take the lead when the time is right, with a strong connection to both the world and to spiritual awareness.

MY COLOR | WHITE

WHITE represents relaxed confidence that allows complete trust and surrender.

Reflect on the color white, a color we see when all wavelengths of light are perfectly and equally balanced.

FRUIT OF MY ESSENCE | KIWANO

Also known as a horned melon, the kiwano is an otherworldly-looking fruit native to sub-Saharan Africa. With a vibrant orange and somewhat spiky skin, the inside is filled with yellow and green seeds, the vibrant flesh tasting like lemony cucumber. Like a Six, the spikes, warm color and appeal keep danger away, but the complex interior is actually a harmonious, almost gelatinous, beautiful blend of citrus and heavenly flavors. A fruit of the earth and heavens.

HAVE A "RELAXING FUN" DAY OR EVEN A "RELAXING FUN" HOUR

What do you do for fun? This question perplexes many Sixes, who have difficulty just having fun and relaxing. Adrenalizing activities, if you do them, may stimulate you, but being adrenalized is not the same as relaxing. Discover what is fun and relaxing for you, then spend a day doing only these things. If you are not ready for a full day, then practice this for one hour and keep increasing the amount of time you allow yourself to relax and do so on a regular basis, at least once a month.

ASK YOURSELF THESE FOUR QUESTIONS

When you have a thought that concerns you – and remember that it is just a thought – ask yourself these four questions and in this order:
Is this thought true?
How do I know if it's true?
What else could be true?
What is my perspective now?
You might want to write down your answers. Repeat this line of self-questioning every time a thought appears that causes you concern.

LEARN HOW TO TRUST YOUR INTUITION MORE

Because you have a continuously operating antenna you are likely quite insightful and even intuitive. At the same time, what you are picking up may actually be inside you, a projection of your own thoughts, concerns, feelings and more. How do you know the difference between a true intuition and a projection? An intuition has no emotion of any kind associated with it. Projections are laden with many emotions. So, if what you are thinking is emotion free, it is likely an intuition and you can trust it. If your thought is fraught with emotion, it is likely to be a projection of your own inner state. If your thought has some emotion but not intense ones, it is likely both an intuition and a projection. In this case, you can sort out what part is the projection and then explore these thoughts and feelings by asking yourself: *In what ways are these thoughts and feelings actually inside me? What remains after this self-exploration is most likely intuition.*

6

"For my entire life, I've worried and anticipated, but I thought this was what most people do. At the same time, I tried to hide my level of uncertainty from others because I didn't want them to see me as an anxious, unconfident or pessimistic person. I'm actually not pessimistic at all; I'm really more idealistic, hoping for the best and planning against that – problem solving in advance – so obstacles don't impede the good. All the pre-planning also helped me feel prepared and safer, since I knew what to expect, or so I thought. Two things changed that. One was an excellent coach who has never told me I was making things up. The coach listens, then asks this simple question: *How does that thought serve you?* The second thing is something my sister said. She said that instead of inserting myself in the movie I was creating in my mind, what if I could just sit back and watch the movie? I do that quite often now, even bringing in imaginary popcorn!"

We are all capable of handling life's challenges

I can overcome fear through the courage to take fully conscious action

ENNEAGRAM SEVEN

THE JOYFUL PERSON

I'm an Enneagram Seven! I am highly energetic, exciting, enthusiastic, and engaging. Many people say I am also charming, but I think it's really that I love new people, novel ideas, and unusual experiences. These things stimulate me and keep me going in a very positive way. I guess my enthusiasm can be contagious. I move around a lot, talk — and think — faster than most people, and love to have fun. Why not? I always think *Why not* rather than *What if*. Why be downtrodden when you can be upbeat? Stimulation, excitement and pleasure are what motivate and sustain me. I really do believe that everything is possible. Really, there's no reason to limit yourself. In fact, thinking there are limitations is what causes limits in the first place. When other people try to limit me, I get rebellious.

7

*I looked inwards
And the beauty of
my own emptiness
Filled me until dawn
~ Rumi*

MY LIFE MOTTO
There are infinite possibilities in this life; we should experience as many of them as we can.

WHY THIS RUMI POEM?
Sevens have a relentless need for a continuously changing variety of external stimulation as a way to both feel full and to not experience the emptiness they often feel inside. Rather than settle for momentary and everchanging temporary fulfillment from the outside, this poem reminds Sevens to pursue the inward journey, the path of true satisfaction.

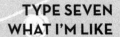

WHAT I LIKE

Infinite possibilities, freedom, options, high energy, new ideas, fascinating people, learning new things, unlimited choices, positivity, pleasure, stimulation, variety and excitement

WHAT I DISLIKE

Pessimism, the word 'NO,' people who complain, feeling limited, negativity, repetition and routine, being told what to do, feeling trapped, slowness, boring people and pain of any kind

I feel like it is my job to keep everyone, including me, upbeat, energized and positive, and I constantly try to make this happen. It does get tiring sometimes, but it is well worth it.

I SEARCH FOR STIMULATION AND PLEASURE

I AVOID PAIN AND DISCOMFORT

FAVORITE SONGS

"Happy"
~ Pharrell Williams

"Celebration"
~ Kool & the Gang

"Let's Get the Party Started"
~ Pink

FAVORITE SPORT | GYMNASTICS

Gymnastics has it all: a variety of events, plus it requires grace, artistry, flexibility and agility, all of which I love. Add to that the sense of you're almost flying, feet off the ground suspended in air. Plus, you can do it in so many ways: on your own, in groups, in competitions and you can do it just for the fun of it if you want.

7

FAVORITE ACRONYMS

TL;DR | too long; didn't read

YOLO | you only live once

WOOT | hooray!

MY MUSICAL INSTRUMENT | ALTO SAXOPHONE

The alto saxophone is an amazing instrument ... a sound that can't be tamed or constrained ... has numerous finger keys ... possibilities for playing are endless ... good for classical, jazz, pop, whatever ... did you know that Charlie Parker played the alto saxophone ... how cool is that!?

WHAT IS EASY FOR ME

Having fun, seeing the bright side of just about anything, being playful, starting something new and exciting, being creative, being flexible, generating an abundance of new ideas myself, brainstorming new ideas with others, and changing course mid-stream or even at the end

WHAT IS HARD FOR ME

Being focused, being still for any period of time, dealing with feelings – mine or others – for very long if at all and especially pain or sadness, feeling restrained or constrained, being around people who are slow or pessimistic, feeling bored, and completing tasks on time

I believe that time is just a mental construct which is always negotiable; we are all free spirits, although most people don't recognize this.

MY ESSENTIAL OIL | EUCALYPTUS

Exhilarating, uplifting and energizing, lifting the mind and spirit into possibilities

EUCALYPTUS OIL

"I just kind of wake up with new ideas every day, and I follow that dream, as they say."

~ **Dolly Parton**

77

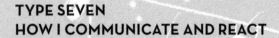

VERBAL CUES

» Fast, spontaneous speech
» Upbeat word choice and tone
» Tell engaging stories

NONVERBAL CUES

» Bright, excited eyes
» Smile continuously
» Highly animated

MORE ABOUT HOW I COMMUNICATE

» I make and share quick connections between things that others may not easily grasp.
» I don't use punctuation or complete sentences all the time; why bother?
» For me, listening means I hear what you say and add ideas when you are still talking; this shows I'm interested but you may think I'm interrupting.
» I lose interest very easily when someone is talking if they are boring or I already know what they are going to say (and I usually do).
» I make jokes a lot or do other things to relieve tension when things get too serious.

"Joy comes to us in ordinary moments. We risk missing out when we get too busy chasing down the extraordinary."

~ Brené Brown

7

HOW I BEHAVE WHEN ANGRY

» Avoid the situation by thinking of pleasurable alternatives
» Rationalize by reframing my own behavior so it is positive, not negative
» Blame or even condemn others when I am extremely upset and feel I have no available exit strategy

MY HOT BUTTONS

» Boring, mundane, repetitive tasks
» Lack of stimulation
» Not being taken seriously or feeling restricted
» Any kind of criticism, but especially unjust criticism
» Not having my ideas heard
» Being forced to focus on negative issues and problems

HOW I AM WITH CONFLICT

I do not like conflict at all and escape from it using a variety of escape hatches, mostly trying to reframe what occurred to cause the conflict. At the same time, I am told that I generate conflict by being late, not completing tasks on other people's time schedules, and more. Causing conflict is not my intention.

HOW I BEHAVE WHEN STRESSED

» Become anxious
» Can be excessively talkative or extremely quiet
» Hyper-manic with extreme or prolonged stress
» Depressed if I can't get out of it
» Can get highly anxious and far more in touch with my fear than normal
» Sad although I may not know why
» Become both angry and blaming

MY STRESSORS

» Feeling trapped in any way: job, life, relationships, rules, tasks and commitments
» Not being listened to or taken seriously
» Having my ideas not fully considered
» Hurting or offending someone I care about and not knowing it
» Feeling sad or hurt
» Authority figures asserting their role-based or personal authority and restricting or chastising me

FEAR is my underlying emotional state, but I am an expert at running away from my fear – and most other feelings except joy – by going into my head and conjuring up exciting, pleasurable and stimulating ideas. Really, my mind is always active and so intriguing that whenever I feel fear, boredom, sadness or anything that causes me pain or discomfort, I go into my mind and all is well. This works the vast majority of the time. My thoughts look much like a fractal: lovely, exciting, and unpredictable in a good way. A fractal has no ending and no boundaries, just like my mind. In fact, my mind moves so quickly from one thing to another, or one idea to something else connected to it, that I am never, ever bored by my own thoughts. Did you know that a fractal is a continuously repeating pattern found in most natural things such as rivers, seashells, clouds and more? And an abstract fractal can also be generated by a computer, displaying a beautiful visual that is actually a simple equation repeated over and over again.

SEVEN
HAIKU

Excitement and sounds

Ideas concepts movement

Crave stimulation

HOW I DEAL WITH MY FEAR
Primarily I don't feel fear very much at all because if and when I do, I instantaneously go into behavior that takes me as far from fear as possible. This can be thought of as positive possibility thinking or planning. I also move quickly from fear by doing something new or something that captures my interest. Some people say that I am constantly 'chasing the next new shiny object' that comes my way and, believe me, new objects appear constantly and instantaneously, be they people, sounds, something visual, and more. My lack of focus on any one thing for very long – combined with my need to be perpetually stimulated – is just another way to avoid most feelings, including fear.

3 WAYS OF DEALING WITH MY FEAR THROUGH STAYING EXCITED, STIMULATED AND UPBEAT

Which version or combination am I?

3 SUBTYPES OF ENNEAGRAM SEVEN

Each version or subtype of Seven deals with staying excited, stimulated and upbeat in a different way

KEEPERS OF THE CASTLE | SELF-PRESERVATION SUBTYPE

Staying stimulated and energized by forming networks – a protective castle – of family, friends and colleagues to keep myself secure, but also to generate new and exciting opportunities

SACRIFICE | SOCIAL SUBTYPE

Staying stimulated and excited through group engagement to share ideas and new learnings; momentarily sacrificing my direct pleasure for the needs of the group, but wanting to be acknowledged and thanked for this

FASCINATION | ONE-TO-ONE SUBTYPE

Keeping upbeat and stimulated by living in an embellished reality of a super-positive, almost a romantic, dream-like state

MY AFFIRMATION
"I AM WHOLE"

Breathe so that this affirmation goes beyond just thought; allow your heart and whole body to experience this affirmation.

MY ANIMAL | BUTTERFLY

Of course, the butterfly as it so beautifully lilts from flower to flower, always with grace and ease, as if its wings could allow it to fly anywhere. But the butterfly is also a symbol of magnificent adaptability, with both an ability and an attraction to metamorphosis. The bringer of joy and peace, floating above most earthly matters, the butterfly is also a symbol of profound transformation.

MY COLOR | YELLOW

YELLOW is the color of the kind of joyful curiosity that comes from being in the moment, in the now.

Reflect on the color yellow.

FRUIT OF MY ESSENCE | RAMBUTAN

Behold the rambutan, an outrageous looking, hairy red fruit that looks more like something out of a fairy tale than anything from real life. Like a Seven, inside the rambutan, with its exotic shell, dispersed energy and hard-to-miss exterior, lies its smooth, almost poetic inner fruit, with a stillness that is close to perfection and a pure interior, delicious to the taste.

SLOW DOWN BY USING YOUR BREATH

Maybe you've never thought about this or maybe you have! You actually breathe primarily into your head area and perhaps into your neck, but not much below that. Your short and rapid head-based breathing goes quickly and both matches and creates your very fast-paced energy. To slow down more, which would be good for you to do, first just notice the way you breathe without changing anything. Next, as you breathe, simply allow your breath to go gently a little deeper. Then, allow your breath to gradually go deeper still. Doing this breathing activity incrementally makes it easier to do. Keep gently allowing deeper breathing. You will definitely slow down a bit and get more oxygen in your system as well. More oxygen will help relax you and increase your sense of well-being.

GROUND YOURSELF FROM YOUR HEAD DOWN TO YOUR FEET

Being and feeling grounded helps us feel centered, whole and aligned. Have you ever noticed that your energy is so high, your feet may not feel they are on the ground? Literally, of course, your feet are on the ground. But figuratively, you may not feel connected to the earth. Instead of learning how to ground yourself starting with your feet, Sevens do better grounding starting at the top of their heads and then moving their awareness and energy down to their feet, making sure to not skip any part of their body as they move downward. You can do this visually through imagination or somatically through your senses. Do this activity until you feel like you 'get it,' enjoy the process and the journey, and then do this every day at least once a day. It's short and fun, but also so beneficial.

SPEND ONE DAY IN COMPLETE SILENCE

This is an amazing adventure and you do it with no phones, no emails, no text messages, no social media activity and no in-person conversations of any kind! Simply be with you for one entire day (24 hours) in complete silence. Of course, you can do things, but everything is done without talking or writing: silence! Your family and friends can support you in this if you explain what you are doing and why. Explain that you are doing this to spend more time exploring what is occurring inside you. It is best to do this silent day alone, but if that is not possible, it's OK if others say something to you. Just don't talk or write in response. What will you discover? Wait and see, but here's a hint. You'll be able to see the patterns of your thoughts, and you'll start to explore your interior world in an entirely different way.

"It's been said about Enneagram Sevens that they have to 'hit the wall' in order to really change because Sevens can make anything, and I mean anything, that is at all negative into something positive. I would share the story of my growing up as if it were a happy family, when it was anything but. I was absolutely abused physically and psychologically, but it was too painful to face. So I retold myself that all was good and even believed it. Eventually, this story and many others like it, felt hollow. And when I went to explore what also felt hollow inside me, a space that I was trying to fill with 'fun' things, I found a depth of sorrow and anxiety I could not have imagined. Harder for me still is to access my anger, but I can do it with help from others. It is my path to being whole and complete."

7

True joy and happiness comes from being able to fully focus at will

I am satisfied and whole because I have integrated both pain and pleasure

ENNEAGRAM EIGHT

THE POWERFUL PERSON

I'm an Enneagram Eight! Some people say I am a force to be reckoned with and that my big energy can be felt even when I am saying and doing nothing. I have a keen sense when things are chaotic or out of control – often before others perceive this – and then step in to take charge. If things are well under control in an effective way, I step back, although I do like a little chaos and will sometimes stir the pot, just to make sure something is happening. I have a big heart, although I often keep it hidden, and I am quick to anger, although I see anger as simply energy, a vitality that then leads to action. I love action, big action and also impact, big impact. My gut instincts are strong and trustworthy; I get an immediate sense of someone and quickly, within seconds, decide whether this is a trustworthy individual. Forward moving, I like things big and bold.

8

*There is a
sacredness in tears
They are not the mark
of weakness
But of power
~ Rumi*

MY LIFE MOTTO
The world is divided into the strong and the weak; I must be among the strong.

WHY THIS RUMI POEM?
Eights believe that showing vulnerability of any kind is weakness, firmly believing that strength is good and weakness of any kind is bad. But when they allow the tears of vulnerability to emerge and then integrate this aspect of themselves, they learn that true strength includes being vulnerable: strength through vulnerability.

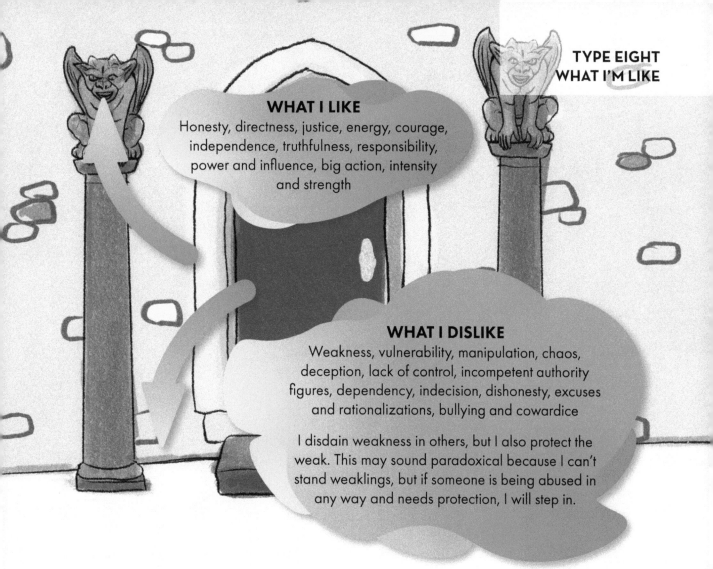

WHAT I LIKE

Honesty, directness, justice, energy, courage, independence, truthfulness, responsibility, power and influence, big action, intensity and strength

WHAT I DISLIKE

Weakness, vulnerability, manipulation, chaos, deception, lack of control, incompetent authority figures, dependency, indecision, dishonesty, excuses and rationalizations, bullying and cowardice

I disdain weakness in others, but I also protect the weak. This may sound paradoxical because I can't stand weaklings, but if someone is being abused in any way and needs protection, I will step in.

I SEARCH FOR CONTROL AND JUSTICE

I AVOID FEELING VULNERABLE OR WEAK

FAVORITE SONGS

"Respect"
~ Aretha Franklin

"Steamroller Blues"
~ James Taylor

"I Can't Get No Satisfaction"
~ Rolling Stones

FAVORITE SPORT | SUMO WRESTLING

A full-contact, entirely competitive sport, it involves both superior strength and strategy. You either force your opponent out of the circular ring or force them to the ground, usually by throwing, shoving or pushing. The sumo wrestler is highly respected, but the respect is earned based on merit, not based on role.

FAVORITE ACRONYMS

TBH | to be honest

WTF | what the f***

GR8 | great

MY MUSICAL INSTRUMENT | DRUMS

Drums, of course! What else would you expect? With power and force, and the ability to modulate my tone, my job is to keep the beat so that other instruments and vocalists follow my lead. Monkeys drum objects as a form of social dominance. Drums are also used by the military to call attention, keep control, motivate the troops and send signals to battling warriors. Drummers keep the beat; the beat controls the rhythm of the entire song!

8

WHAT IS EASY FOR ME
Being strategic, protecting others, being bold, taking charge, exerting control, feeling potent, being grounded, asserting myself, saying what I think, and intimidating others when necessary

WHAT IS HARD FOR ME
Feeling vulnerable, being receptive, asking for assistance, relying on other people, being flexible, not knowing what to do, changing my perception of someone if initially negative, and feeling fully gratified

Although I typically take what I want and don't understand why others don't do this as well, at a deeper level, I rarely feel fully satisfied.

MY ESSENTIAL OIL | CEDARWOOD
Aromatic and woodsy, with powerful uses as an antiseptic, anti-inflammatory and diuretic

CEDARWOOD OIL

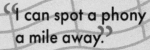

"I can spot a phony a mile away."

~ Dolly Parton

VERBAL CUES
» Use profanity and body-based humor
» Short, simple sentences
» Give commands

NONVERBAL CUES
» Authoritative with strong physical presence
» Grounded, almost immovable
» Direct eye contact

MORE ABOUT HOW I COMMUNICATE
» I get right to the point; don't waste my time and I won't waste yours.
» I know how to modulate my tone and volume to get the impact I want.
» I don't like to communicate with low-energy, passive people.
» People say they can sense my presence and power even when I say or do absolutely nothing.
» Four letter words are part of my everyday language, and I use them frequently.

"Vulnerability is not weakness. And that myth is profoundly dangerous."

~ Brené Brown

HOW I BEHAVE WHEN ANGRY

- » Feel intense surges of anger that propel me to fast action
- » Quickly sift and sort through the situation and my reactions
- » Avoid feeling vulnerable or out of control
- » May withdraw entirely
- » May seek the counsel of individuals I trust and respect
- » Dismiss and discard reactions of people I do not respect

MY HOT BUTTONS

- » Indirectness
- » Deception
- » Injustice
- » Others not taking responsibility for their behavior
- » Being blind-sided
- » Not feeling in control

HOW I AM WITH CONFLICT

Some people think I like conflict; this is not true. I don't like or dislike conflict, but I will deal with it quickly and directly when it occurs. I am not afraid of it. In addition, what others perceive as conflict, I often experience as passionate and honest conversation.

HOW I BEHAVE WHEN STRESSED

- » Become more excessive in a variety of ways – overeating, extreme exercise, insufficient sleep, workaholism, constant shopping
- » May take big action even faster than usual
- » Become aggressive, withdrawn or both
- » Get insistent, controlling and punitive
- » Might become sick and deeply discouraged

MY STRESSORS

- » Feeling out-of-control
- » Feeling blind-sided or sabotaged
- » Feeling betrayed or hurt by someone I've trusted
- » Unintentionally hurting someone I care about
- » Having my territory or authority challenged
- » Allowing myself to be vulnerable or to need someone, then being abused
- » Perceiving someone as cruel, unjust or unfair

ANGER is my underlying emotional state, and that's OK with me. I actually think of anger, for the most part, as an energy or vitality that propels me to action. I'd describe it more as an expression of my passionate nature than just anger. It also helps me set clear boundaries for myself in relationship to others. When I say 'NO,' I mean 'NO.' There is no confusion about this. Some people say that they get intimidated by my big energy and especially so when I am angry. Intimidating others this way is not necessarily my intention, so I try to modulate the expression of my anger, sometimes with success and sometimes not. But when I keep it in, I can get sick or implosive, neither of which is good. Energy management has been a lifelong challenge. Am I too big? Is this my problem or is it the other person's? I am willing to confront injustice and poor behavior directly in terms of fighting, although not necessarily a physical fight. More often, I prefer the super-hero-strategy. I can save the person or the city with my pure strength, and this is often enough to have people stop what they are doing.

HOW I DEAL WITH MY ANGER

This could be put two different ways. People have to deal with me with my anger, or that's what I've always thought. But I also have to learn to deal with my anger, which actually serves to hide or cover deeper emotions that I associate with feeling vulnerable, which I detest feeling. When I feel sad, I get angry. When anxious, I get angry. When I feel angry, I get really angry. And whenever I feel angry, my anger propels me to take immediate action; this also discharges the intensity of my anger so I don't internalize it. In addition, I also use feeling powerful and being excessive as a way to deal with my big energy that is anger-fueled.

EIGHT HAIKU

Large truth and power

Make important things happen

Protecting people

3 WAYS OF DEALING WITH MY ANGER THROUGH BEING POWERFUL AND EXCESSIVE

Which version or combination am I?

3 SUBTYPES OF ENNEAGRAM EIGHT

Each version or subtype of Eight deals with power and excessiveness in a different way

SURVIVAL | SELF-PRESERVATION SUBTYPE

An excessiveness in going after what is needed for survival, in part by scanning for, engaging in, and directing and controlling important power and influence networks

SOLIDARITY | SOCIAL SUBTYPE

Vigorously and excessively protecting others and challenging social norms and systems, and being powerful enough to continuously organize, lead and protect groups where I am in charge

POSSESSION | ONE-TO-ONE SUBTYPE

Being excessively rebellious and provocative, passionate, and powerful in being able to control and dominate people and events

MY AFFIRMATION
"I AM PURE"

Breathe so that this affirmation goes beyond just thought; allow your heart and whole body to experience this affirmation.

MY ANIMAL | LION

Although the lion is king of the jungle, the lion also represents heart and courage. With majesty and strength, lions are natural-born leaders with a deep sense of authority and the ability to overcome just about any difficulty, especially those that are more challenging to navigate. The lion is also about being in charge, but a reminder that this is really about being in charge of yourself — your emotions as well as your actions, rather than trying to take charge of the world. It is about following your heart.

MY COLOR | RED

RED is the color of vitality, passion and intensity that comes from being fully human, with strength and vulnerability intertwined.

Reflect on the color red.

FRUIT OF MY ESSENCE | GUANÁBANA

Its spiky exterior and massive size — individual fruits weigh up to 11 pounds — can seem intimidating, but don't be in fear of the guanábana. Inside is a different story. The slippery white flesh melds the flavors of pineapple and banana, with a floral aroma and a texture like ice cream. Like the guanábana, Eights hide their sweet and vulnerable parts beneath their bold exterior. Good mixed with juices or delectable raw, when ready and ripe, both guanábanas and Eights feel soft to the touch and delicious to eat.

TAKE BETTER CARE OF YOUR PHYSICAL WELL-BEING

You likely drive yourself very hard and do very little in moderation. For example, of course you eat, but do you tend to over-eat or under-eat, binge eat or any of the above in alternating fashion? Try to go for consistent, healthy eating. What about exercise? Do you exercise at all? If you do, do you go in spirts, where you exercise a lot and then not at all? What about sleep: hardly any sleep or do you go to bed really late so you can have the night to yourself, but then don't get enough sleep in the morning? These are all ways of being excessive – something too much or too little or both – rather than being more moderate. Being more moderate and rhythmic with your self-care will increase your physical well-being and support your being less reactive and more receptive.

REFLECT ON THE NATURE OF VULNERABILITY

Become philosophical and ask yourself some challenging questions: *Is vulnerability really weakness? Who have I known or observed who was able to be both very strong and show vulnerability? Is my reluctance to be vulnerable actually coming from a place of fear, and if so, what am I afraid of?* These are hard questions, but the answers can be illuminating.

SLOW DOWN YOUR IMPULSE TO TAKE ACTION

Every time you feel an impulse to take action, which is likely often, imagine a pause button inside you and push it. Take a breath while you do this and ask yourself this question: *What am I actually feeling underneath this desire to act. Fear? Hurt? Anger? Excitement? Lack of control? Deep disappointment? Frustration? Desire?* Once you determine the feeling, ask yourself this: *And what am I feeling this way about?* Explore your answer. Once you've paused enough to address these above questions, you'll have more insight. And then, if you still want to take action, you certainly can do so! However, you will have slowed down your process, which can help you make even better decisions.

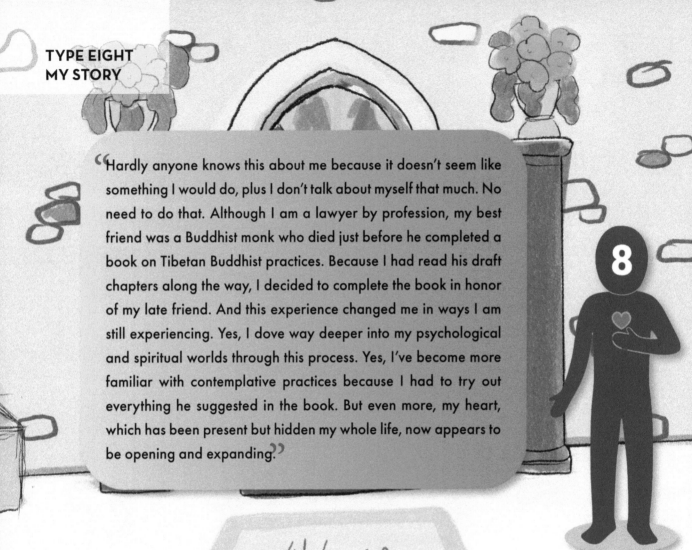

"Hardly anyone knows this about me because it doesn't seem like something I would do, plus I don't talk about myself that much. No need to do that. Although I am a lawyer by profession, my best friend was a Buddhist monk who died just before he completed a book on Tibetan Buddhist practices. Because I had read his draft chapters along the way, I decided to complete the book in honor of my late friend. And this experience changed me in ways I am still experiencing. Yes, I dove way deeper into my psychological and spiritual worlds through this process. Yes, I've become more familiar with contemplative practices because I had to try out everything he suggested in the book. But even more, my heart, which has been present but hidden my whole life, now appears to be opening and expanding."

8

Welcome

The truth comes from being fully open to and integrating multiple perspectives

I am innocent, pure and receptive

ENNEAGRAM NINE

THE PEACEFUL PERSON

I'm an Enneagram Nine. I'm very low-key and really like harmony. I love when there is no tension, no conflict, everyone's needs are getting met, and everyone feels that their voice is important. I am very easy-going, relaxed, and non-judgmental, at least compared to other people. Inside, I may be more judgmental and tense than I appear from the outside. I'm told I'm easy to talk to and quite approachable, and I often get involved in helping others mediate or reconcile their differences. I can even do this without having those involved in a conflict talk to each other. Why? Because they feel like I listen to their perspectives and support them. Sometimes I'm supposed to do something, but don't. I may forget what it was. Sometimes, I just didn't want to do it, but didn't know how to say 'No' to that person without creating tension between us. I've been known to be a bit messy — my room, my desk — but I can find everything I want.

9

MY LIFE MOTTO

It's OK, you're OK; I think I'm OK; we're all OK if we just listen to each other and get along.

*You must ask for
what you want
Don't go back to sleep
The door is round
and open
Don't go back to sleep
~ Rumi*

WHY THIS RUMI POEM?

Nines are known as 'anger that went to sleep,' and this has many meanings. Nines keep their anger so minimal that they often don't recognize it. Without access to their anger, however, Nines also put their entire vibrancy to sleep, lose their 'voice' and become disabled from knowing and expressing what they want. The poem's message is this: "Wake up and let your voice be heard!"

WHAT I LIKE
Peace, harmony, positive regard, mutual respect, inclusion, routine, comfort, humility, people who listen well, everyone having a voice and being heard, and relaxing

WHAT I DISLIKE
Anger, conflict, tension, rudeness, being pressured, aggressiveness, arrogance, pretentiousness, ambitious people, rudeness, being controlled, ego-centrism, and people who don't listen well

Although I look as if I am highly tolerant of everyone, I really don't like people who are rude, pushy or exclusionary.

I SEARCH FOR HARMONY AND COMFORT

I AVOID DIRECT CONFLICT AND ILL WILL

TYPE NINE
INTERESTING THINGS ABOUT ME

FAVORITE SONGS

"Watching the River Run"
~ Loggins and Messina

"Sittin' On the Dock of the Bay"
~ Otis Redding

"Everything's Gonna' Be Alright"
~ Bob Marley

FAVORITE SPORT | CURLING

What's the point of curling, a 42-pound stone pushed down the ice, while two players sweep in front of the stone to get the stone to curl or move? What's the point of any sport? With curling, it's the slow process that's fascinating! Even more, the goal is for the stone to get closest to the target, called a "house." Ah, the comfort of home. Physicists still don't know what puts the curl in curling.

MY MUSICAL INSTRUMENT | XYLOPHONE

With a light, playful sound, my volume might not be as loud as other instruments. Some people don't take me seriously because I can be moved around so easily, but I am actually quite versatile – for example, as part of an orchestra or as a stand-alone instrument. If you listen closely, you will notice that there is subtle, elegant power to my sound, blending melodically and harmoniously with so many other instruments. And I don't call too much attention to myself.

FAVORITE ACRONYMS

IMHO | in my humble opinion

NTIM | not that it matters

FUTAB | feet up take a break

9

WHAT IS EASY FOR ME
Developing rapport, relaxed conversations and small talk, listening to what others say, noticing that someone hasn't been included, being agreeable, not making waves, not calling attention to myself, and making people feel comfortable

WHAT IS HARD FOR ME
Accessing and expressing my own opinions and desires, being assertive, focusing on myself, dealing with conflict unless I am mediating, and experiencing strong feelings of any kind, especially anger

What's really hard for me is to express my opinions, wants, and needs. Either I don't know what they are or I do know, but don't say anything so as to avoid tension. Sometimes I know what I don't want, so I can then back into what I do want.

MY ESSENTIAL OIL | LAVENDER
Calming and relaxing, used in bathing since the ancient Egyptians and Romans

LAVENDER
OIL

"My philosophy is simple: It's a down-home, common sense approach to things."

~ Dolly Parton

VERBAL CUES
» Give highly detailed information
» Use agreeing words like uh huh
» Share information in sequence from first to last

NONVERBAL CUES
» Minimal facial tension
» Easygoing demeanor
» Relaxed posture

MORE ABOUT HOW I COMMUNICATE
» I am a very good listener, showing and verbalizing affirmations and being able to understand all points of view.
» I don't get too upset about anything, so my responses tend to be moderate and even-tempered.
» I like to 'schmooze' or engage in pleasant conversations with people about a variety of topics; this helps build rapport and is very relaxing.
» I am extremely diplomatic in how I help people resolve issues.
» When I feel angry, which is rare, I may take a nap to relax myself.

9

"We cannot selectively numb emotions; when we numb the painful emotions, we also numb the positive emotions."

~ Brené Brown

102

HOW I BEHAVE WHEN ANGRY

» Usually say nothing and energetically withdraw
» Facial tension may give a slight indication of anger
» May be entirely unaware that I'm angry
» Displace anger onto someone or something not directly involved
» May feel angry for long periods of time
» Experience a great deal of internal physical tension
» Can become passive-aggressive

MY HOT BUTTONS

» Unresolvable disharmonious situations
» Chronic complainers
» Rudeness
» Others not being seen or heard
» Not feeling seen or heard myself
» Anger that is directed at me
» Feeling pressured or directed to do something

HOW I AM WITH CONFLICT

I don't like feeling angry or when someone is angry at me. However, I am adept at helping others resolve conflicts. I am a good listener, believe in resolving issues without making anything personal, and enjoy restoring harmony between individuals and groups.

HOW I BEHAVE WHEN STRESSED

» Become quiet, highly talkative or both
» Feel physically tense
» Experience insomnia or sleep deprivation
» Become more defused and forgetful than normal
» Become irritable, stubborn or refuse to do things
» Engage in secondary activities as a way to soothe myself, relax more and reduce the pressure

MY STRESSORS

» Feeling angry
» Someone being angry with or threatening me
» Feeling pressured to do something I don't want to do
» Falling behind in my responsibilities and tasks
» Someone taking advantage of me
» Not feeling my voice has been heard or my opinions honored

ANGER is my underlying emotional state, but I hardly ever get angry. When I do get upset, I become extremely distressed. Anger, in my view, can destroy the harmony in human relationships that is so important. I don't know which I dislike more, when I feel angry or when someone else is angry with me. When I get angry, I am often not very aware of it; I keep these feelings and sensations so deep below the surface that I often don't feel them. And if I do feel distressed, I do something I enjoy to relax myself and dissipate my anger: walk the dog, go online, engage in a hobby, or binge-watch a show, even if I've seen it many times before. I also collect things, although I don't always perceive these collections as helping me deal with anger. However, they actually do. These collections bring me comfort and pleasure, and they restore an internal sense of peace. I get very tense when someone gets angry with me; it upsets me. I am so agreeable and accommodating, what's to get mad about?

HOW I DEAL WITH MY ANGER

Essentially, I deal with my anger by not dealing with my anger. I do this in a number of ways. I lose full contact with my body – my somatic experiences – so I don't have many body-based cues of anger, such as a heat starting in the bottom of my gut that gets bigger as it rises. I use my mind to say to myself things such as "It's not a big deal, so let It go," or "It doesn't really matter; don't say anything." If I do start to feel angry, my anxiety rises, and this keeps me from expressing my anger. But the primary way I deal with my anger is to diffuse my attention so my anger rarely arises. I diffuse my attention by merging or blending with something outside myself, thus losing myself in the process.

NINE HAIKU

Harmony and peace

Dislike conflict and ill will

Easy going smile

3 WAYS OF DEALING WITH MY ANGER THROUGH BLENDING AND MERGING

Which version or combination am I?

3 SUBTYPES OF ENNEAGRAM NINE

Each version or subtype of Nine deals with blending and merging in a different way

APPETITE | SELF-PRESERVATION SUBTYPE

Diffusing my attention by blending and merging with comforting, rhythmic and pleasurable activities and routines as a way of losing touch with myself

PARTICIPATION | SOCIAL SUBTYPE

Diffusing my attention by blending and merging with groups, working hard on their behalf as a way to belong and not focus on myself

FUSION/UNION | ONE-TO-ONE SUBTYPE

Diffusing my attention by blending and merging with one other person – or a series of others – as a way of not paying attention to myself and my own feelings, needs and desires

MY AFFIRMATION
"I MATTER"

Breathe so that this affirmation goes beyond just thought; allow your heart and whole body to experience this affirmation.

MY ANIMAL | SLOTH

The sloth represents embracing the small pleasures in life, the importance of modesty and tranquility, and living in peace and harmony with the rest of all living things. In addition, sloths symbolize patience and grace, connection and community. They also serve as a reminder to not worry about the small things that are unimportant and to find balance in your life, including the need for being silent and still with finding your voice and taking action.

MY COLOR | DAYLIGHT

DAYLIGHT is the color of being so fully awake that you are deeply engaged in everything and touched by all that you experience.

Reflect on the color daylight.

FRUIT OF MY ESSENCE | MANGOSTINO

The rind, an earth-like body color, is both beautiful and hard to access, hiding a white interior with a delicious flesh. As with Nines, experiencing what is inside is worth it, but not always easy to get to. Inside you'll find something sweet and smooth, with ambrosial qualities. A mangostino tree can grow as tall as 80 feet or 25 meters, but you can't hurry its development. It can take three years to even reach a height of one meter. Similarly, Nines take their own time to grow and change, but when they are ready, the results are remarkable and well worth the wait.

EXPRESS YOUR PREFERENCES DIRECTLY

You can start with something very basic such as what you want to eat. Imagine that someone asks you this: *What would you like to have for dinner?* Most Nines say, *I don't know. What would you like to have for dinner?* The other person might say, *Chinese food.* The Nine says, *I don't really like Chinese food.* The other person then says, *Well, what do you like?* And the Nine then says, *It doesn't really matter. What do you like to eat?* And so the conversation continues like this when Nines are asked what they want. Instead of saying, *I don't know,* try saying, *Let me think for a moment.* Then either go inside yourself and ask what kind of food you really do want. If you don't know, ask yourself what kind of food you don't want and then back into what you do want. Then share your answer.

SAY HELLO TO YOUR ANGER

Anger can become your friend if you are willing to say 'hello' to it. You don't have to act on it unless you choose to, but it is important to notice when you are angry about something. Getting more in touch with your anger will help you set boundaries with others and enable you to say 'No' when that's what you feel, instead of automatically saying 'Yes.'

ENGAGE IN A FULL BODY SCAN

You don't need an X-ray or an MRI, just yourself. Once a day, or more if you like, start anyplace in your body and ask yourself, *What do I experience in my body here?* Then move to another area of your body, close to where you began and ask the same question. Continue this process throughout your entire body. If there is no answer to your question, just notice that and move to another area, repeating the same question. Some people find it easier to start at their head and move down. Others prefer to start at their feet and move upward. Choose whatever works best for you. Doing this daily supports your body awareness and somatic intelligence. In addition, it helps you get in touch with physical sensations and emotional feelings. In other words, it can help 'wake you up.'

9

9

"I really don't like talking about myself that much, but I'll get straight to the point, although I usually like to give lots of context. When I was working for the government, I discovered someone was embezzling money from my department. What to do? Report it and get into all kinds of conflict and turmoil? You know what happens to people who 'blow the whistle' on wrongdoing. I abhor conflict. Forget about it, which I couldn't do. Or quit my job? With incredible support from one person in my life, I made a huge decision to report the problem while they investigated, plus I stayed on the job. Three horrible and stressful years later, they concluded I was, in fact, right so all the hardship I endured was vindicated. But the real impact was that I had found my voice, stood up for principle, and had been transformed by it. Now, I can stand up straight, have deep access to my desires and feelings, and am willing to tell you what I want. What an amazing journey!"

There is underlying unconditional regard and love in the world

I have an embodied presence so I know what I want and what action to take

LAST CHAPTER

> "Between stimulus and response there is a space. In that space is our power to choose our response. In our response lies our growth and our freedom."
>
> **~ Viktor Frankl**
> Neurologist, psychiatrist, author and Holocaust survivor

How do you create the space between stimulus and response so that you have more freedom to choose how you respond and are not responding out of habit and reactivity? How can you best observe your Enneagram type in action – including your thoughts, feelings and behavioral responses?

Self-observation is the answer and involves 6 sequential steps. Remember that self-observation is a choice, one that will lead you to greater freedom and possibility.

This 6-step PAUSE-PLAY can be repeated over and over again until it becomes more natural and ongoing. The more you do it, the more your self-awareness increases, your self-acceptance accelerates, your self-development heightens and your newly found freedom of choice launches you into new ways of being and unexpected possibilities.

STEP 1 | PUSH PAUSE
WHEN TO PUSH PAUSE
- Self-observe at any time.
- Self-observe in the midst of your reacting to something.
- Self-observe after something has occurred.

HOW TO PUSH PAUSE | Take 3 breaths to create the space.

MAKE THE CHOICE TO BE SELF-OBSERVING

STEP 2 | SELF-OBSERVE
WHAT SHOULD I OBSERVE FOR?
- Anything that arises and grabs your attention
- Thoughts, feelings and behaviors as they emerge
- Specific type-based thoughts, feelings and behaviors

NOTICE WHAT YOU OBSERVE WITHOUT JUDGMENT

STEP 3 | SELF-REFLECT
WHAT SHOULD I SELF-REFLECT ABOUT?

THE 3 QUESTIONS
- What are my patterns of thoughts, feelings and behaviors?
- Where do my patterns come from?
- Do my patterns still serve me?

GIVE YOURSELF TIME TO REFLECT

STEP 4 | CONSIDER CHOICES
WHAT CHOICES DO I HAVE?

THE 3 QUESTIONS
- What are my options?
- Are there additional options?
- Which options are the most viable?

THINK IN TERMS OF POSSIBILITY

STEP 5 | CHOOSE
CHOOSE ONE OPTION

THE 3 QUESTIONS
- Which option gives the greatest potential benefit?
- Which option has the greatest potential risk?
- Which option do I really want to try?

STEP 6 | PRESS PLAY
SEE WHAT HAPPENS

THE 3 QUESTIONS
- How did that go?
- What were the consequences?
- Would I want to do that again?

PRACTICE THE PAUSE-PLAY CYCLE AGAIN

APPENDIX

APPENDIX A

QUESTIONS TO CONFIRM YOUR TYPE

You may already know your type at this point, but if not, these three questions regarding each Enneagram type may be useful. If you are this type, you'd likely answer yes to all three questions or, at least, two out of the three questions.

AM I A ONE?

» Do I have an inner voice – akin to a tape recorder in my head – that continuously criticizes me for what I do wrong and sometimes applauds me when something goes exceedingly well?

» Do I have a constant need for self-improvement, while knowing that no one will ever be perfect, not even me?

» Do I have a hard time relaxing and having fun unless I am on vacation and away from my responsibilities?

AM I A TWO?

» Do I intuitively know what someone else needs but have a hard time articulating my own needs, even to myself?

» If I'm completely honest, do I believe that I can get almost anyone to like me if I really want to?

» Do I feel really good when others respond to me in the way that I most want, but particularly deflated when this does not occur?

AM I A THREE?

» Do I constantly do things to impress others so that they will value and respect me?

» Am I so busy 'doing' things that I don't even know what simply 'being' means?

» Do I avoid failure by engaging only in activities I think I will be good at?

AM I A FOUR?

» When I feel something strongly, do I hold onto my emotions intensely for extremely long periods of time, continuously replaying my thoughts and feelings?

» Do I think of melancholy as a wistful experience?

» Do I continuously search for deep connections with others and feel distraught when these connections become severed?

AM I A FIVE?

» When a situation gets emotional or intense, do I automatically disconnect from my feelings in real time, then reconnect with some of these later on?

» Do I primarily observe life rather than being fully engaged in it?

» Do I create an invisible boundary between myself and others so that other people understand they should not approach me unless invited to do so?

AM I A SIX?

» Do I regularly anticipate multiple scenarios, thinking about what could go wrong and trying to plan so that this will not occur?

» Do I have strong positive or negative reactions to authority figures and try to befriend them, adhere to what I think they want, or challenge them when I am concerned?

» Do I project my thoughts and feelings onto others, having difficulty discerning whether something is really occurring or whether I am creating it in my mind?

AM I A SEVEN?

» Do I continuously seek new and stimulating people, ideas, or events to keep life exciting, stimulating, and forward moving?

» Do I avoid pain and discomfort whenever possible, using my mind to conjure up new possibilities and plans and to reframe negative situations so they can be seen as positive?

» Do I have trouble sustaining my focus on work projects, people, and conversations without a considerable amount of effort on my part because I get so easily bored and distracted?

AM I AN EIGHT?

» Do I have an extraordinarily strong and bold exterior, one that is sometimes intimidating to others but that hides a less visible, highly vulnerable interior?

» Do I tend to be excessive in what I do – for example, exercising two to three hours a day for a week but then not exercising for a month, or deciding that if one piece of chocolate cake is good, then eating the whole cake is even better?

» Do I have immediate impulses to take strong and forceful action, particularly when I am feeling anxious or vulnerable?

AM I A NINE?

» Do I automatically blend or merge with other people's positive energy, but get distressed when I am around negativity, anger, and conflict that can't be resolved?

» Do people find me easy to approach and nonjudgmental in almost all circumstances?

» Do I have great difficulty expressing my opinions, particularly if they may be controversial in some way or could create conflict?

APPENDIX B

TYPE CONFUSIONS AND CLARIFICATIONS

People can get confused between two different types and here's why.

» Some types engage in similar behaviors, but they do so from different inner motivations.

» People can become confused between their actual type and a wing or arrow of that type; wings are types on either side of a type, while arrows point toward and away from each type.

» Sometimes, a subtype – one of the three versions of a type – can resemble another type.

The following charts will help you understand some of the distinctions between each pairs of types.

TYPE ONE	TYPE TWO
Task oriented	Relationship oriented
Self-controlled	At ease
Polite	Friendly
Internally focused	Externally focused

TYPE ONE	TYPE THREE
Want to be right	Want to be effective
Highest quality only	High quality if possible
Highly structured	Flexible structure
Internally oriented	Externally oriented

TYPE ONE	TYPE FOUR
Prefer precise standards	Prefer self-expression
Like rules	Like latitude
Highly structured	Minimalist structure
Follow the gut and head	Follow the heart

TYPE ONE	TYPE FIVE
Self-controlled	Self-contained
Prefer doing	Prefer thinking
Work extra hours	Adhere to time boundaries
Involved	Detached

TYPE ONE	TYPE SIX
Believe there is one right way	Believe in multiple pathways
Restrained	Intense
Plan from the gut	Plan from the mind
Certain	Ambivalent

TYPE ONE	TYPE SEVEN
Constrained	Spontaneous
Disciplined	Emergent
Reserved	Engaging
Diligent	Distractible

TYPE ONE	TYPE EIGHT
Focus on detail	Focus on big picture
Self-controlled	Unconstrained
Suppress anger	Express anger
Micro-manage	Macro-manage

TYPE ONE	TYPE NINE
State opinions	Don't state opinions easily
Direct	Indirect
Judgmental	Accepting
Tense	Relaxed

TYPE TWO	TYPE THREE
Want to be liked	Want to be respected
Focus on purpose	Focus on goals
Patient with emotions	Impatient with emotions
Want to help	Want to impress

TYPE TWO	TYPE FOUR
Focus on others' feelings	Focus on own feelings
Presume they'll be liked	Fear they'll be rejected
Try to understand others	Want to be understood by others
Help others not suffer	Explore own suffering

TYPE TWO	TYPE FIVE
'False' abundance perspective	'False' scarcity perspective
Emotional	Logical
Move toward people	Move away from people
Warm	Cool

TYPE TWO	TYPE SIX
Worry about people	Worry about most things
Concerned with relationships	Concerned with risk calculation
Seek appreciation	Seek support
Do for others to be liked	Do for others out of loyalty

TYPE TWO	TYPE SEVEN
All feelings OK	Only positive feelings OK
Can stay attentive	Easily distracted
Want to be liked	Want to be stimulated
Focus on others	Focus on self

TYPE TWO	TYPE EIGHT
Make decisions from heart	Make decisions from gut
Repress anger	Express anger
Exert indirect control	Exert direct control
Subtle	Bold

TYPE TWO	TYPE NINE
Like to intuit what others need	Like to be told what others need
More emotional	More even-tempered
Energetic	Easygoing
Move toward people	Let others come to them

TYPE THREE	TYPE FOUR
Want to be seen as successful	Want to be seen as unique
Driven by goals	Driven by inner passion
Focus on task	Focus on feelings
Prefer emotional restraint	Prefer emotional expression

TYPE THREE	TYPE FIVE
Results oriented	Knowledge oriented
Push feelings to the side	Disconnect from feelings
Read audience well	Not focused on others' response
Engage with others easily	Prefer time alone

TYPE THREE	TYPE SIX
Relish results	Relish planning
Don't show inner anxiety	Express inner anxiety
Plan for few obstacles	Plan for multiple obstacles
Self-composed	Intense

TYPE THREE	TYPE SEVEN
Focus easily	Distracted easily
Plan for action	Plan for possibility
Like several options	Like infinite options
Want admiration	Want stimulation

TYPE THREE	TYPE EIGHT
Overly care what others think	Unconcerned with what others think
Practical results	Big results
Conforming	Rebellious
Seek validation	Seek influence

TYPE THREE	TYPE NINE
Perceive relaxing as being idle	Relax easily
Like quick action	Prefer deliberative action
Driven	Easygoing
Confident	Humble

TYPE FOUR	TYPE FIVE
Show emotions	Keep emotions private
Trust the heart	Trust the mind
Subjective	Objective
Try to connect with others	Try to keep distance from others

TYPE FOUR	TYPE SIX
Emotionally intense	Mentally intense
Not focused on risk	Calculate risk
Scrutinizes self	Scrutinizes others
Defy tradition	Adhere to tradition

TYPE FOUR	TYPE SEVEN
Emotionally intense	Emotionally light-hearted
Engage sorrow	Avoid sorrow
Relish feelings	Relish ideas
Internally focused	Externally focused

TYPE FOUR	TYPE EIGHT
Believe they won't get what they want	Go after what they want
Make decisions from the heart	Make decisions from the gut
Concerned about feelings	Concerned about influence
Want others to connect	Want others to take responsibility

TYPE FOUR	TYPE NINE
Intensely emotional	Emotionally low key
Like deep talk	Like small talk, schmoozing
Emotions fluctuate	Emotionally even tempered
Like intense interactions	Prefer non-intense interactions

TYPE FIVE	TYPE SIX
Deal with fear through withdrawal	Deal with fear through anticipatory scenarios
Remote	Intense
Seek knowledge	Seek security
Prefer distance from others	Engage with others

TYPE FIVE	TYPE SEVEN
Sequential, logical mind	Synthesizing, non-sequential mind
Non-intense energy	High energy
Experience fear privately and reflectively	Avoid fear through pleasurable pursuits
Relish solitude	Relish constant stimulation

TYPE FIVE	TYPE EIGHT
Uncertain sense of personal power	Heightened sense of personal power
Somatically non-intense	Somatically intense
Live in a world of information	Live in a world of big action
Disconnect from all emotions in real time, including anger	Express anger as it emerges

TYPE FIVE	TYPE NINE
Let others know when to approach	Highly approachable
Dislike small talk	Like small talk to develop rapport
Seek knowledge	Seek harmony
Disconnect from others	Merge with others

TYPE SIX	TYPE SEVEN
Doubting mind	Synthesizing mind
Ask 'what if...?' questions	Make 'why not...?' statements
Plan for what could go wrong	Expect everything to go right
Idealistic realists	Perpetual optimists

TYPE SIX	TYPE EIGHT
Make decisions with the mind	Make decisions with the gut
Need and ask for support	Difficulty asking for support
Hyper-vigilant thru the mind	Attentive, but through the gut
Feel pressured by others	Demanding of others

TYPE SIX	TYPE NINE
Tightly wired	Relaxed
Intense	Light-hearted
Anticipate problems	Overlook problems
Reactive	Non-reactive

TYPE SEVEN	TYPE EIGHT
Light energy	Intense energy
Value the mind	Value the gut
Optimistic	Realistic
Seek freedom	Seek control

TYPE SEVEN	TYPE NINE
Tell stories starting from own interest, then skip around	Tell stories sequentially from start to finish
High energy	Low to moderate energy
Seek excitement	Seek peace
Express their desires	Don't express desires

TYPE EIGHT	TYPE NINE
Express anger directly	Express anger indirectly
Get straight to the point	Explain context as way to get to the point
Control by taking charge	Control by not letting others control them
Use demand and command	Use consensus and compromise

APPENDIX C

THE ENNEAGRAM'S ARCHITECTURE

For those of you who benefit from and enjoy understanding frameworks, the Enneagram is a coherent framework describing the 9 architectures or ego structures of what it means to be human. To explain this, think of a metaphor of a bird representing each type. Think of the bird as the person, with type being the most important feature or aspect. Then, there are multiple other components of type as you can learn about below: wings and arrows, fixations and holy ideas, passions and virtues, and subtypes: Self-preservation (SP), Social (S), and One-to-one (1-1). The Enneagram architecture sits in the context of the three Centers of intelligence: Body, Heart and Head.

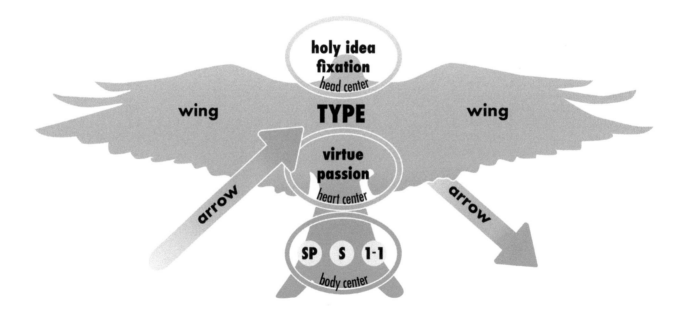

TYPE
WHAT IS A TYPE AND WHY IT MATTERS

Enneagram type is the fundamental framework of the 9 different human ego structures that make us human. It is this very humanness in each of us that leads us on our unique path to self-understanding and self-acceptance, compassion for ourselves and others, and to our most profound self-development and transformation.

CENTERS OF INTELLIGENCE
WHAT ARE THE CENTERS OF INTELLIGENCE AND WHY THEY MATTER

All of us have three Centers of Intelligence – Body Center, Heart Center and Head Center – and each Center has specific functions: deeply truthful somatic or gut knowing for the Body Center; balanced emotions and compassionate relating for the Heart Center; and objective and insightful reasoning for the Head Center. Each Enneagram type tends to use each Center of Intelligence in type-specific ways, some of which are productive and support our growth and some ways that keep us limited. Knowing your type accurately helps you understand the ways in which you use and don't use your Centers effectively; knowing this information is extraordinarily helpful as a guide to your growth through developing your ability to use your Centers in the most productive ways.

In addition, the 9 Enneagram types can also be divided into three sets of three, with three types being formed in each Center of Intelligence and each Center being associated with a primary human emotion: Body Center – types 8, 9 and 1 – formed as three different responses to anger; Heart Center – types 2, 3 and 4 – formed as three different responses to sorrow; and Head Center – types 5, 6 and 7 – formed as three different responses to fear. These type distinctions based on the Centers of Intelligence and their common emotion can be seen on the following chart:

BODY CENTER TYPES	3 Enneagram types formed in response to anger
TYPE 8	Readily express anger; believe anger is simply energy that needs to be released
TYPE 9	Avoid own and others' anger; adept at mediating conflict with others to restore harmony
TYPE 1	Manifest anger as irritation and resentment; believe anger is a negative emotion

HEART CENTER TYPES	3 Enneagram types formed in response to sorrow (sorrow from not being true self)
TYPE 2	Create an image of being likeable, generous and concerned for others
TYPE 3	Create an image of being competent, confident and successful
TYPE 4	Create an image of being unique, special and different

HEAD CENTER TYPES	3 Enneagram types formed in response to fear
TYPE 5	Withdraw due to fear of both intrusion and complete depletion of energy
TYPE 6	Develop scenarios to minimize risk and fear or embrace risk to prove their fearlessness
TYPE 7	Avoid fear by engaging in positive possibility thinking and staying constantly stimulated

WINGS AND ARROWS

WHAT ARE WINGS AND ARROWS AND WHY THEY MATTER

Wings are the two types on either side of your type, thus their name wings. While they do not change your core type, they can add certain qualities to make you more resourced and robust. Some people utilize both wings, some use neither wing, and some people use one wing more than the other.

Arrows refer to the two types that are connected to your type by the arrows on the Enneagram symbol. As with wings, arrows do not change your core type, but they can add certain qualities to make you more resourced and robust.

TYPE	WINGS	ARROWS
1	NINE wing | More relaxed, consensual, less reactive TWO wing | More generous and people-oriented	FOUR arrow | More emotional and creative SEVEN arrow | More fluid, spontaneous and fun-loving
2	ONE wing | More detailed and task-driven THREE wing | More comfortable being visible and high-profile	EIGHT arrow | Deeper personal power and bolder FOUR arrow | Increased emotional depth and creativity
3	TWO wing | More generous and attuned to others' feelings FOUR wing | More emotional, deeper personal presence	NINE arrow | More relaxed and mellow SIX arrow | More analytical and insightful
4	THREE wing | More action oriented and higher energy FIVE wing | More objective and analytical	TWO arrow | Warmer and more attuned to other people ONE arrow | More detail-oriented and discerning
5	FOUR wing | More emotional and aesthetic SIX wing | More team oriented and loyal	SEVEN arrow | More playful and spontaneous EIGHT arrow | More powerful and action-oriented
6	FIVE wing | More internally focused and self-contained SEVEN wing | More optimistic and higher energy	THREE arrow | More certain and confident NINE arrow | More relaxed and flexible
7	SIX wing | More perceptive and careful EIGHT wing | More assertive and powerful	ONE arrow | More detail oriented and follow-through FIVE arrow | More reflective and quiet
8	SEVEN wing | More lighthearted and adventurous NINE wing | Less reactive and more consensual	FIVE arrow | Quieter and more self-reflective TWO arrow | Warmer and more open-hearted
9	EIGHT wing | More take-charge and forceful ONE wing | More attentive and discerning	SIX arrow | More insightful and deliberative THREE arrow | More goal-focused and forward moving

FIXATIONS AND HOLY IDEAS

WHAT ARE FIXATIONS AND WHY THEY MATTER

Each type has a repeating MENTAL habit or pattern of THINKING that goes with that type. Fixations matter because they both reflect the type and also reinforce it. Because of this, understanding your type-based fixation enables you to self-observe your thoughts and thought patterns more astutely and to work on this area as a key to your self-development. We can change the way we think as a way to change ourselves if we want to do so.

WHAT ARE HOLY IDEAS AND WHY THEY MATTER

The holy ideas, one specific to each Enneagram type, are the non-fixated, higher states of mind for that type. They are aspirational and inspirational, but they also offer fully possible transformed ways of being for each type. They represent more of who we truly are in our deeper self or essence. At a deep level, we already know these holy ideas to be true. They can be used in a variety of ways for our growth and transformation: as mantras for us to repeat and remind ourselves of what is really true and who we are; as precious moments we experience in our lives so that we can remember these states and re-experience them over and over during self-reflection; and as areas for deeper contemplation.

TYPE	FIXATIONS (MENTAL PATTERNS)	HOLY IDEAS (HIGHER SPIRITUAL STATE)
1	**RESENTMENT** Chronically paying attention to flaws so that nothing ever seems good enough	**HOLY PERFECTION** Knowing that everything is as it should be and that even imperfection is perfect
2	**FLATTERY** Paying attention to how to gain acceptance through giving compliments or other forms of attention	**HOLY FREEDOM • HOLY WILL** Knowing that acknowledging oneself and one's own needs leads to autonomy and freedom
3	**VANITY** The strategic thinking about how to create an idealized image based on being or appearing to be successful	**HOLY HOPE • HOLY LAW • HOLY HARMONY** Belief that you can be valued for yourself and who you are rather than what you do or accomplish and that there is a natural order and flow
4	**MELANCHOLY** Thinking continuously about what is missing, with accompanying thoughts of being disconnected or separated from others	**HOLY ORIGIN • HOLY SOURCE** Knowing that nothing is missing and that everyone and everything are deeply connected because we all emanate from the same source
5	**STINGINESS** A scarcity paradigm that leads to an insatiable thirst for knowing, a reluctance to share – knowledge, space, personal information – and strategizing about how to control your environment	**HOLY OMNISCIENCE • HOLY TRANSPARENCY** Knowing that only through direct personal experience and full engagement can all things be known
6	**COWARDICE** Thoughts of doubt and worry that cause the creation of worst-case or anticipatory scenarios	**HOLY STRENGTH • HOLY FAITH** Believing that both you and others can capably meet life's challenges and that there is certainty and meaning in the world
7	**PLANNING** The mental process by which the mind goes instantly into "hyper-gear," moving in rapid succession from one thing to another	**HOLY WORK • HOLY PLAN • HOLY WISDOM** Directing your mental focus to the important work at hand, sustaining that focus without distraction, and knowing we are all part of a bigger plan
8	**VENGEANCE** The process of rebalancing the score or achieving justice though thoughts related to anger, blame and intimidation	**HOLY TRUTH** The ability to seek and integrate multiple points of view in search of the higher, deeper and bigger truth
9	**INDOLENCE** Mentally diffusing your attention so you forget what is important and refrain from expressing your preference and opinions, thereby minimizing conflict with others	**HOLY LOVE** Knowing there is an underlying universal harmony in the world based on unconditional regard and appreciation for one another

PASSIONS AND VIRTUES

WHAT ARE PASSIONS AND WHY THEY MATTER

Each type has a repeating EMOTIONAL habit or pattern of FEELING that goes with that type. Passions matter because they both reflect the type and also reinforce it. Because of this, understanding your type-based passion enables you to self-observe your feelings and feeling patterns more astutely and to work on this area as a key to your self-development. We can change the way we feel as a way to change ourselves if we want to do so.

WHAT ARE VIRTUES AND WHY THEY MATTER

Each Enneagram type also has a type-specific virtue, a higher state of emotional response for that type. Virtues are also aspirational and inspirational, but they also offer fully possible transformed ways of being for each type. They represent more of who we truly are in our deeper self or essence. At a deep level, we already know these virtues. They can also be used in a variety of ways for our growth and transformation: as mantras for us to repeat and remind ourselves of what is really true and who we are; as precious moments we experience in our lives so that we can remember these states and re-experience them over and over during self-reflection; and as areas for deeper contemplation.

TYPE	PASSIONS (EMOTIONAL PATTERNS)	VIRTUES (HIGHER SPIRITUAL STATE)
1	**ANGER** The feeling of chronic dissatisfaction with how things are	**SERENITY** An openhearted acceptance to all that occurs
2	**PRIDE** Inflated and deflated self-esteem and self-importance derived doing for, being needed and being liked by others	**HUMILITY** Feelings of self-acceptance and self-worth without either self-inflation or deflation based on the reactions of others
3	**DECEIT** Feeling you must do everything possible to appear successful, hiding parts of yourself that do not conform to that image, and believing that your image is the real you	**TRUTHFULNESS** Finding true self-acceptance through acknowledging both your success and failures, realizing that your image is not your essence
4	**ENVY** Consciously or unconsciously comparing yourself to others on a continuous basis, with accompanying feelings of deficiency, superiority, or both	**BALANCE** Experiencing your inner state in such a clear and centered way that thought, feeling and action emanate from your inner self
5	**AVARICE** The intense emotional desire to guard everything related to oneself – information, privacy, energy, and resources – combined with automatic detachment from feelings	**NONATTACHMENT** The first-hand understanding that detachment is not nonattachment and that you must fully engage in something before you can become nonattached
6	**FEAR** Feelings of anxiety, deep concern, and panic that the worst will occur, that others can't be trusted, and that you are not up to the challenges that present themselves	**COURAGE** The feeling of being capable of overcoming fear through clear and fully conscious action, rather than turning to either inaction or action designed to prove you have no fear
7	**GLUTTONY** The insatiable, unrelenting and instantaneous emotional thirst for new stimulation of all kinds – people, ideas, things and experiences	**SOBRIETY** Feeling full, complete and satisfied as a person, which comes from pursing and integrating painful and difficult experiences as well as pleasurable and stimulating ones
8	**LUST** A desire for excessiveness in a variety of forms – for example, work, food, pleasure – as a way of avoiding and denying feelings and vulnerabilities	**INNOCENCE** The childlike feeling of vulnerability and openness, such that the need to control situations or protect oneself and others is no longer present
9	**LAZINESS** Lethargy in paying attention to your feelings and needs, thus disabling you from speaking your truth and taking desired action	**RIGHT ACTION** Being so fully present to yourself and others that you know exactly what action to take

SUBTYPES | 3 versions of each type

WHAT ARE SUBTYPES AND WHY THEY MATTER

Subtypes represent three sub-versions of each type, thus the name subtype. They are formed when the passion of each type combines or intersects with one of the basic human instinctual drives that is activated in you – for self-preservation, for social community or for one-to-one intimacy. The type-based passion then alters the instinct so that the true needs in that instinctual domain get thwarted and distorted.

Knowing your subtype – and you may be a combination of more than one subtype of your type – matters for several reasons. First, knowing your subtype may help clarify your Enneagram type; the subtype descriptions may be a more nuanced description of your type in action. Second, because your subtype response is when you are most in the throes of your automatic type-based behavior, this can assist you in self-observation. Third, knowing your subtype can help you target your type-based development more precisely.

You can see the 3 basic human instincts below:

SELF-PRESERVATION INSTINCT

Physical existence, safety, security, danger, resources, structure and control

SOCIAL INSTINCT

Belonging, community, groups, social relationships, and influence.

ONE-TO-ONE INSTINCT

Self in relation to one other person, affection, intimacy, bonding and attraction

THE THREE BASIC INSTINCTS

When you have one of these instincts more active in you, it does not mean you are good at getting your needs met in that arena or that you necessarily like that area of life. It means that your attention and energy go most consistently toward that area, away from it, or that you have the most ambivalence about that aspect of life. In many people, two of these instincts may be active, although these instincts may appear at different times in our lives or in different circumstances – for example, at home versus work.

Each of the 27 Enneagram subtypes, the three versions of each type, has a unique name; these subtypes are referred to in the earlier book sections for each type. Here they are repeated again, plus the earlier page number where they can be found.

TYPE *PASSION*	SELF-PRESERVATION SUBTYPE	SOCIAL SUBTYPE	ONE-TO-ONE SUBTYPE	PAGE NUMBER
ONE *ANGER*	WORRY	NON-ADAPTABILITY	ZEAL	9
TWO *PRIDE*	ME-FIRST • PRIVILEGE	AMBITION	AGGRESSION • SEDUCTION	21
THREE *DECEIT*	SECURITY	PRESTIGE	MASCULINITY • FEMININITY	33
FOUR *ENVY*	RECKLESS • DAUNTLESS	SHAME	COMPETITION	45
FIVE *AVARICE*	CASTLE	TOTEM	CONFIDENCE	57
SIX *FEAR*	WARMTH	DUTY	STRENGTH • BEAUTY	69
SEVEN *GLUTTONY*	KEEPERS OF THE CASTLE	SACRIFICE	SUGGESTIBILITY • FASCINATION	81
EIGHT *LUST*	SURVIVAL	SOLIDARITY	POSSESSION	93
NINE *LAZINESS*	APPETITE	PARTICIPATION	FUSION • UNION	105

APPENDIX D

LEVELS OF SELF-MASTERY FOR EACH TYPE

If you wonder why people of the same type can, in some ways, appear to be so different, there are many reasons for this – for example, usage of wings and arrows, predominant subtype or subtypes, but also contextual and environmental factors such as early formative experiences, family overlays, cultural overlays, and more. In addition to all these factors, people of the same type can differ in terms of their level of self-mastery. Self-mastery, sometimes called levels of development, refers to a number of factors related to a person's capacity in these areas: self-awareness, emotional self-regulation, making effective choices, resilience under duress, interpersonal relationships, and more.

Self-mastery level – but also a person's highest range of self-mastery when they are at their best and their lowest level when are under duress – explains why people of the same type might appear to be functioning differently from one another. Low self-mastery is fear-based; medium self-mastery is concern-based; and high self-mastery is wisdom-based. Our current self-mastery level shows us not only where we are on the self-development trajectory, but also the direction in which we need to grow.

HIGH SELF-MASTERY | WISDOM-BASED

High self-awareness, high emotional self-regulation, act out of choice rather than habit or impulse, high resilience with the ability to learn and thrive from duress, relate extremely well to a variety of other people

MEDIUM SELF-MASTERY | CONCERN-BASED

Intermittent self-awareness, some degree of emotional self-regulation, make some effective choices and some out of habit, moderate resilience to survive duress, relate well to some people but not others

LOW SELF-MASTERY | FEAR-BASED

Low self-awareness, emotionally reactive with minimal self-regulation, behave out of habit rather than choice, low resilience or the ability to bounce back from duress, relate poorly to most people

TYPE ONE | HIGH SELF-MASTERY

Dignified, patient, peaceful, accept people and things as they are, joyful, spontaneous

Core Wisdom | everything and everyone is perfect as they are, including imperfections

TYPE ONE | MEDIUM SELF-MASTERY

Discerning, opinionated, reactive, highly organized, structured, detail-focused, easily irritated

Core Concern | making a mistake and being imperfect

TYPE ONE | LOW SELF-MASTERY

Intolerant, inflexible, tightly wound, volatile, highly critical, highly judgmental, unforgiving

Core Fear | being bad and having something deeply and intrinsically wrong with them

TYPE TWO | HIGH SELF-MASTERY

Purely and deeply generous without any expectation, gentle and humble, solid sense of inner well-being

Core Wisdom | a profound purpose exists for everything that happens, independent of anyone's efforts

TYPE TWO | MEDIUM SELF-MASTERY

Warm, read others well, flattering of others, emotional, difficulty saying 'no,' give abundant advice

Core Concern | feeling valuable, being liked, feeling needed, appreciated and worthy

TYPE TWO | LOW SELF-MASTERY

Manipulative, shaming, despairing, guilt-inducing, deeply angry, take no responsibility for own behavior

Core Fear | being unwanted, discarded and intrinsically unworthy

TYPE THREE | HIGH SELF-MASTERY

Know and express who they are at a deep level, express what they feel, admit their foibles, deeply genuine

Core Wisdom | everyone has intrinsic value for who they are; there is a natural flow to everything

TYPE THREE | MEDIUM SELF-MASTERY

Focus on goals, plans and activity, driven, competitive, seek recognition, limited time for relationships

Core Concern | being successful, avoiding failure, gaining respect from others

TYPE THREE | LOW SELF-MASTERY

Inauthentic, contrived, opportunistic, self-serving, aggressive, isolated, deep inner emptiness and grief

Core Fear | extreme fear of both failure and having no value

TYPE FOUR | HIGH SELF-MASTERY

Centered, balanced, calm, grateful, consistent, compassionate, manifest fully without hesitation

Core Wisdom | everything and everyone has meaning and significance and is deeply connected

TYPE FOUR | MEDIUM SELF-MASTERY

Dramatic or withdrawn, constant search for depth and meaning, sensitive, expressive, self-reflective

Core Concern | feeling significant, special and finding meaning

TYPE FOUR | LOW SELF-MASTERY

Bitter, depressed, emotionally volatile, extremely angry, hyper-sensitive, deeply wounded, ashamed

Core Fear | being intrinsically defective and completely disconnected

TYPE FIVE | HIGH SELF-MASTERY

Fully experience feelings in real time, lively, spontaneous, imaginative, integrated, fully accessible

Core Wisdom | true wisdom involves the integration of first-hand experience from head, heart and body

TYPE FIVE | MEDIUM SELF-MASTERY

Aloof, private, detached from feelings in real-time, keep needs minimal, guard time, energy and autonomy

Core Concern | conserving resources, guarding privacy, feeling competent through gaining knowledge

TYPE FIVE | LOW SELF-MASTERY

Frightened, withdrawn, isolated, highly secretive, cut off from feelings, constantly strategizing

Core Fear | being helpless, incapable, depleted, overtaken and harmed by others

TYPE SIX | HIGH SELF-MASTERY

Insightful, intuitive, calm, resilient, courageous, confident, trusting, honor own inner authority

Core Wisdom | meaning and certainty exist both inside ourselves and outside ourselves

TYPE SIX | MEDIUM SELF-MASTERY

Perceptive, overly busy, endearing, seek certainty, approval seeking, rebellious against unjust authority

Core Concern | belonging, safety, and being able to trust both self and others

TYPE SIX | LOW SELF-MASTERY

Extreme anxiety, frenzy, continuous worst-case scenario thinking, clingy, reject disagreement, paranoid

Core Fear | having no support or sense of meaning and being unable to survive

TYPE SEVEN | HIGH SELF-MASTERY

Focused energy, listen thoroughly, calm and vital, complete work with joy, inspire by their presence

Core Wisdom | genuine happiness and wholeness come from integrating negative and positive experiences

TYPE SEVEN | MEDIUM SELF-MASTERY

Creative, engaging, unfocused, reframe negative events into positive ones, need constant stimulation

Core Concern | satisfaction, stimulation, feeling free, feel good

TYPE SEVEN | LOW SELF-MASTERY

Highly anxious, alternate being manic or distressed, joyless, blaming, feel cornered and trapped

Core Fear | pain, deprivation, not feeling whole, having no escape

TYPE EIGHT | HIGH SELF-MASTERY

Manage big energy effectively, acknowledge vulnerability, generous, receptive, warm, deeply confident

Core Wisdom | true strength includes vulnerability, multiple truths must be heard and integrated

TYPE EIGHT | MEDIUM SELF-MASTERY

Protective, controlling, bold, constantly take immediate action, require bigger and bigger challenges

Core Concern | self-protection and showing any kind of weakness

TYPE EIGHT | LOW SELF-MASTERY

Direct to the point of cruelty, excessive anger, punishing, extreme power-orientation, antisocial behavior

Core Fear | being harmed, controlled or feeling vulnerable and weak with no protection

TYPE NINE | HIGH SELF-MASTERY

Take stands easily, active and purposeful, engaged, vibrant, alert, with a strong and constant inner core

Core Wisdom | everyone matters, unconditional regard and love connect everyone and everything

TYPE NINE | MEDIUM SELF-MASTERY

Seek peace, harmony and comfort no matter what, mediate differences well, forget what matters

Core Concern | stability, harmony, being heard

TYPE NINE | LOW SELF-MASTERY

Inattentive to self, low energy, ignore issues, neglectful and forgetful, immovable, passive-aggressive

Core Fear | separation from others, being controlled, anger, conflict

ADDITIONAL RESOURCES

BOOKS BY GINGER LAPID-BOGDA PHD

Bringing Out the Best in Yourself at Work (2004) | core work applications of the Enneagram

What Type of Leader Are You? (2007) | develop leadership competencies using the Enneagram

Bringing Out the Best in Everyone You Coach (2010) | high-impact coaching using the Enneagram

The Enneagram Development Guide (2011) | 50+ development activities for each type

Consulting with the Enneagram (2015) | a systematic structure for achieving powerful results

The Enneagram Coloring Book (2016) | a right and left-brained way to learn the Enneagram

The Art of Typing (2018) | powerful tools for Enneagram typing

BOOK BY GINGER LAPID-BOGDA PHD AND RUSSELL (TRES) BOGDA

The Art of the Enneagram (2020) | in-depth, engaging and highly visual introduction to the Enneagram

BOOKS BY OTHER AUTHORS

Nine Lenses on the World by Jerry Wagner PhD | a psychological perspective on the Enneagram and types

The Complete Enneagram by Beatrice Chestnut PhD | full descriptions of the 27 Enneagram subtypes

The Wisdom of the Enneagram by Don Riso and Russ Hudson | levels of development for each type

Essential Enneagram by David Daniels MD and Virginia Price PhD | easy-to-read psychological overview

APPS

Know Your Type (iOS) | EnneagramApp.com | interactive typing and in-depth Enneagram information

WEBSITES

TheEnneagramInBusiness.com | Ginger Lapid-Bogda's site with resources about the Enneagram, types and applications

EnneagramWorldwide.com | Enneagram in the Narrative Tradition's informational site (Helen Palmer-David Daniels)

TheEnneagramAtWork.com | Peter O'Hanrahan's site with personal and professional Enneagram applications

EnneagramSpectrum.com | Jerry Wagner's site with information about the Enneagram theory, types and applications

EnneagramInstitute.com | Riso and Hudson's site with information about the system, types, and relationships

Conscious.tv | Enneagram type panels interviewed by Iain and Renata McNay

LEARNING PORTAL

Enneagram Learning Portal (ELP) | subscription-based interactive learning with three robust sections: Enneagram, Professionals and Applications | enneagramlearningportal.com

ABOUT THE AUTHORS

GINGER LAPID-BOGDA PHD

As an Enneagram author, teacher and keynote speaker, as well as an organization development consultant, trainer and coach, Ginger works with organizations, leaders, and teams around the globe to create vibrant, productive, and sustainable organizations. ginger@theenneagraminbusiness.com

RUSSELL (TRES) BOGDA

A graduate of UCLA, Tres facilitates Enneagram programs in organizations, coaches individuals, and has an online business selling sports cards. He understands the importance of being whole, integrated and fulfilled, and being mindful and physically healthy, pursuing what you love. tres@theenneagraminbusiness.com

ABOUT THE ILLUSTRATOR

Claire McCracken is Los Angeles-based illustrator and graphic artist specializing in anthropomorphic inanimate objects and all things food-related. She also co-founded Art Mafia, a boutique design firm that specializes in visual art, multi-dimensional exhibits and promoting up-and-coming artists. Find her on instagram @claire_mcc.jpg

ABOUT THE ORGANIZATION

Established in 2004, The Enneagram in Business offers excellent quality, state-of the-art products and services. Why? Because our vision is to help elevate consciousness globally using the Enneagram integrated with other innovative approaches, our mission is to provide an abundance of Enneagram-based resources for use around the world. These include the following:

» Seven Enneagram books, including several best sellers
» Full-color Enneagram training tools, both in hard copy and virtual formats
» Global Enneagram certification programs for consultants, trainers, and coaches
» Premier leadership development and team development offerings
» Training, coaching and consulting services, both virtual and in-person
» A comprehensive, interactive online Enneagram Learning Portal (ELP)
» A global network of top-quality Enneagram professionals (EIBN)

CPSIA information can be obtained
at www.ICGtesting.com
Printed in the USA
BVHW021045041020
590256BV00017B/658

9 781087 908663